Stories from the Porch

Stories from the Porch

Remembrance of a Southern Tradition

Marjorie Morrison Moylan

© 2008 by Marjorie Morrison Moylan.

All rights reserved. No parts of this book may be used or reproduced, stored in a retrieval system, or transmitted, in any form, or by any means, electronic, mechanical, photocopying, recording, or otherwise, without the prior written permission of the publisher.

First edition.

ISBN: 978-0-6151-9916-0

For more information, please contact:
Marjorie Morrison Moylan
300 Deer Valley Road
San Rafael, CA 94903

*D*edicated to

the memory of all the remarkable adults in my childhood
who delighted and intrigued me with their
exciting stories.

*A*ppreciation and acknowledgements
to

My husband Thomas K. Moylan, who gave assurance that others,
beyond family, would find the stories interesting.

Friends in California and Florida who offered encouragement
and astute commentary.

Archives personnel in Florida and Alabama, who not only provided access to
information, but were most gracious and immediate in their responses.

Especially am I grateful to Kay Williams, literary specialist and formatter, who knows
the computer and its workings and improved the appearance and the clarity of a
sentence or paragraph.

Cover design by Ann Rinehart.

CONTENTS

Preface 1

A SUMMER EVENING ON THE PORCH 11

THE BOOKS MUST GO 17

HERE COME THE YANKEES 25

THE MUCH-TRAVELED CONFEDERATE MONUMENT 31

THE MYSTERIOUS DEATH OF UNCLE JOHN............................. 37

THE SUNDAY AFTERNOON CONTEST 47

AUNT BERN'S LEGENDARY PARTIES 53

A TRIP TO TROY 61

THE MANY SUITORS OF NANCY TATOM 69

GOING TO THE GULF 81

STORIES FROM THE PORCH

Preface

As I recall family stories, they were first heard on summer evenings on a porch. Although often repeated versions of another's account, they were nonetheless an important aspect of oral history. While the stories were about persons and events, they also reveal history of the time in which they occurred.

The stories in this collection are those that have remained indelibly impressed on my mind. I heard them on porches in my hometown of DeFuniak Springs, in Northwest Florida: the front porch of my childhood home, Aunt Julia's small porch; my grandmother's veranda and on Aunt Bern's patio; at Grayton Beach on the Gulf Coast thirty miles south of DeFuniak and on Cousin Ethel's ample porch in Troy, Alabama, approximately eighty miles north of my hometown.

The author in front of her childhood home in DeFuniak Springs, Florida.

Southern summer evenings, before air-conditioning, were spent on the front porch of our home on Lake DeFuniak, a perfect circle of one mile around which the town had been founded. On the porch the air was cooler than during the day's steaming temperature. The stars seemed close enough to touch. The moonlight caused the lake to glisten, and fireflies, which we called "lightning bugs," raced madly about from tree to tree.

The "pretty little lake," so described in an early advertising brochure, was the reason for the town's existence. When the L&N Railroad route was planned to connect the

Northwest Panhandle of Florida from Jacksonville to Pensacola, the surveyors were impressed with the beauty of the lake and the surrounding land.

DeFuniak Springs was named for one of the L&N executives. Initially the town with its fine hotel did bring visitors from the North and some remained as permanent residents. But eventually the Scottish pioneers to the area moved from their farms to town and civic leadership became theirs.

Home of author's Morrison grandparents on Lake DeFuniak.

My father's family was one of those. At the turn of the 20th century, his family moved to "town." But, long before that, his grandfather was a leader in opposition to slavery and secession. And his great-grandfather had pioneered the land, living peaceably for decades with his Native American neighbors.

A great-great grandfather, Malcolm Morrison, was one of the first white persons to settle in Eucheeanna. Family lore has it that he and his wife, Margaret Douglass, became friendly with Chief Tampoochee and were buried next to him on the banks of the Choctawhatchee River. A WPA project in the 1930s established a gravesite in honor of Chief Tampoochee, also called Sam Story, in the community of Bruce.

Another setting of stories heard on a porch is at Grayton Beach, thirty miles from DeFuniak Springs on the Gulf of Mexico. This pristine beach of sugar white sand and blue green water was for many years the summer retreat of people from DeFuniak Springs and South Alabama. In the 1930s and '40s there were perhaps twenty cottages on two streets.

One could look down the beach in both directions and not see another person. At no time were there more than a dozen or more people swimming or sunning on the wide beach at Grayton. Today, over-development has caused a change in the appearance of the once quiet beach community. Still, sky and sea, sand and surf are unchanged.

Troy, Alabama, remains the ancestral home of my mother's family of Joneses, Murphrees, and Tatoms. Once heralded as the cultural center of South Alabama, Troy retains its reputation from a fine university, originally the seat of teacher training for the region. In my imagination, Troy became for me an ancient town with very important people. The relatives we met on several occasions were certainly important to my mother and they welcomed us grandly with sincerity and expressions of affection. How we came to rate all this love I didn't know, but it was very nice and different from the more stoic attitude of our Morrison kin.

In the late 1920s and early '30s of my childhood, the Morrisons were secure in their respected positions in the community. Manners and moral values were maintained and I think the former improved through association and marriages to people from the more social South Alabama.

Adding to the delight of the evenings of my childhood would be listening to the exchanges between friends out for a walk around the lake. After a lively greeting, questions would be asked of my father about news, local and national. Even though he had strong views on whatever the topic, his opinion seemed always to be valued.

A quote in an article in *The Washington Post* describes what once took place on porches. "People who sit on porches are making a statement about connecting in their community. A porch bespeaks not only your own place in the world, but also that place from which you reach out to the larger world…it allows you to present yourself to it for encounters with other people."

That's exactly what took place over and over in my growing up years as I observed my father from our porch in DeFuniak Springs greet neighbors or passersby and discuss local and national issues and events.

In the opening story of this compilation, you will hear my father's voice giving his evaluation of politicians, a boxing match and baseball. His take on the progress of the oil well drilling outside of town in the mid-1930s was also a major topic. Another "hot" topic had to do with the chances of getting a bridge across Choctawhatchee Bay and a proposed two-lane road along the edge of the Gulf of Mexico.

On porches in DeFuniak Springs, Grayton Beach, Florida, and Troy, Alabama, I heard stories about the joys and sorrows of the Morrison family, the personalities and experiences of my mother's Alabama Tatom family and stories about the War Between the States, 1861-65, as if it were a recent event.

The Campbell girls on a DeFuniak Springs porch.

Porches in DeFuniak Springs

Bruce House porch looking out on Lake DeFuniak

Walton Hotel porch

First Presbyterian Church

Landmarks of DeFuniak Springs, Florida

Library

Lake DeFuniak

Chatauqua Auditorium

Turn-of-the-century homes in Northwest Florida

Looking at Lake DeFuniak

The Knox Gillis House on Lake DeFuniak

The McConnell House on Lake DeFuniak

The Wesley House, now Eden State Park, Pt. Washington, FL

The Duncan Gillis House on Lake DeFuniak

A SUMMER EVENING ON THE PORCH

Shortly after supper on a warm summer night, my father usually headed for the front porch to read the newspaper in the dwindling light and "watch the world go by." My sister Chris and I trailed after him.

On this early evening it was my purpose to practice dance steps on the sidewalk for a show in which Chris and I had been invited to participate. I didn't get very far with my choreography before a woman and her neighbor, both of whom we knew well, stopped to speak to Daddy. Conversation was always welcomed by my father. He delighted in casual talk and serious debate of issues.

Malcolm Morrison

"Malcolm, what's the news of the oil well today?"

"Flora Douglass, you know I drive out to Rock Hill every day and this afternoon was the most dismal. Everything seemed to go wrong, but the rumor is that John D. Rockefeller's daughter or granddaughter is supposed to be here this weekend and will visit DeFuniak Springs and the oil well. That should be exciting."

"Have her drop a penny in the well for good luck," Flora Douglass replied. "I'm beginning to think nothing's going to come of all that effort. What do you think, Malcolm?"

"Well, you know, I have tried to keep hope in this thing because the Depression is dragging all of us down. Finding oil would make such a difference. But it does seem that one thing after another goes wrong. Times are so hard that yesterday I saw a woodpecker working on a tin roof!"

Midst laughter the ladies waited for Daddy to supply more of his jokes. So he continued.

"And did you hear about the man who paid his

children not to eat supper and then charged them for breakfast?"

"Malcolm, we all need a good laugh. Now we're off to hear the Jack Benny program. See you tomorrow."

"Good-bye, girls," Flora Douglass called to Chris and me.

"Good-bye," Chris answered. "We're practicing our dance for the Kiwanis Club next month."

Actually, Chris and I had stopped still while Daddy and the ladies talked. The practice interrupted, we sat on the steps to the porch and watched the lightning bugs that appear as the daylight fades. Just as we began this familiar activity, Mr. Murray, our next door neighbor, came across the yard.

"Hey, Harry," Daddy called out. "How're you surviving the heat?"

"We've bought an attic fan like I have at the restaurant and the house is cool, cool."

"Harry, you hear a lot of talk at your restaurant. Is it true that the New York Giants may come to Pensacola instead of Cuba next season for spring training?"

"I don't think anybody really knows," Mr. Murray replied. "It's rumored."

Sailors Howard Cawthon and Malcolm Morrison at Key West 1918

"Well, what do you hear about the possibility of a bridge across Choctawhatchee Bay?"

"As you know, Malcolm, that's all up to the Legislature. I would think your brother-in-law is the person to ask. After all, he's been president of the Senate and representing the people of this area for a long, long time."

"Okay, I'll ask him, but you know how he hates to give out information while the Legislature deliberates. I doubt that such a bill will pass. It's gonna' cost a whole lot of money."

"As you know well, Malcolm, if that oil well produces, there will be no problem with getting a bridge across the Bay."

"Harry, I'm banking on that to pull us out of the Depression."

"Hey, Malcolm," a voice from down the street called to Daddy.

"As I live and breathe, is that you, Howard? Never thought I'd see you out for an evening stroll."

"Neither did I," replied Mr. Cawthon, "but Ruth can be pretty persuasive. What I wanted to have you confirm is something I heard on the grapevine. Did you actually refuse an invitation to your sister's dinner party in honor of our Governor?"

"Howard, you know that pompous ignoramus as well as I do from our days at Key West during the War. I wouldn't sit at the same table with him for a million dollars."

"Malcolm, you are one of a kind. Though I know your feelings about the man, still I didn't think you could turn down your sister or Mamie Ruth."

"Don't give it a thought. This will soon be forgotten by anyone who talks of it now. But they could all talk till doomsday and I wouldn't change my position."

"Okay by me. Be seein' you. Remember to salute if he should come this way again."

"You will never see that, Howard!" Daddy called, as Mr. Cawthon and Ruth walked on down the street laughing.

Mamie Ruth Tatom Morrison

Just then Mamma walked out onto the porch. She and Mr. Murray, who had remained quiet during the talk between two old Navy buddies, exchanged greetings. I noticed Mr. Murray repeatedly looking at his watch. Now, he suddenly bid all of us good-night.

My father turned to Mamma, praised how pretty she looked and said, "Mamie Ruth, I know you don't like for the radio to break the quiet of a lovely evening, but I have to hear the Joe Louis fight. Would you mind if I run down to the drug store and listen with the boys gathered there?"

"No, of course not," Mamma replied. "But couldn't we go with you? The girls would love some ice cream on this warm night."

Chris and I began a "please, please" chorus, and I could see Daddy really would like to go by himself, but finally he said, "Okay, let's go."

My father was greeted by loud welcomes. Someone said, "Now, boys, Malcolm's here and you'll hear not only a commentary on this prize fight, but the latest news of the oil well and when Al Smith's coming to town."

"Olin, you know Al Smith will never ever again ride the back of the train to our town only to wind up insulting all of us. A shame, too. He would have made a good president, I think. But thank God for Franklin Roosevelt. I think he'll save the South."

"We have a few minutes before the fight starts. Malcolm, let's hear your opinion of Calvin Coolidge." The men who heard that roared with laughter and anticipation of my father's view, which they knew would be critical but wanted to hear it anyway. He did not disappoint them.

"Well, boys, I think," and he stopped for emphasis, "Calvin Coolidge was the sorriest excuse for a president we have ever had."

"Malcolm," Mamma tried to whisper, "I don't find criticism of the president a subject for the girls to hear." And with that, the three of us, my mother, sister Chris and I walked over to the soda counter for ice cream cones. We could hear the men still talking and laughing, but not shouting anymore. That is, until the fight began and then the noise inside that drug store raised by normally very sedate men drove us outside. It was good to be out in the cool air.

Soon, we were sitting in the car. Chris and I fell asleep so I don't remember hearing the end of the fight on the radio.

"Did Joe Louis win?" I asked as we stumbled out of the car at home.

"You bet he did," Daddy said happily. "That'll be good for all the colored people."

"I'm glad, too," Mamma said. "They need a hero. And won't they be proud?"

"Yes, ma'am, I bet they will," I responded, already thinking about asking the opinion of Cattie, the childhood nurse we'd outgrown but who still worked for us five days a week, preparing meals or cleaning. What I especially loved about Cattie's presence was the records by Louis Armstrong and Clyde McCoy she brought and we played on the Victrola. Oh, tomorrow morning would be fun and maybe I could get the dance steps figured out.

*Chris and Marjorie Morrison
"Dancing with the Daffodils," circa 1930.*

THE BOOKS MUST GO

Introduction

Shortly after the death of my father, Malcolm Morrison, in 1935, his Aunt Jenny came to stay with us. It was from Aunt Jenny that I learned about the Morrison family, about her life in the 1800s. While Aunt Jenny and I shelled peas on the back porch, she talked about her older brothers, Archie and Billy, and about their revered teacher, Mr. Newton.

Reverend John Newton

Mr. Newton, the abolitionist, Amherst educated preacher/teacher imported to teach the children of the Scottish pioneers, was clearly the dominant influence on the people in Walton County. Mr. Newton and the antics of Archie and Billy, as well as the tragedy of their being killed in the War Between the States, became real to me.

What is so ironic and sad about the deaths of Archie and Billy Morrison is the fact of their father's opposition to secession and war. As a delegate to the Florida Secession Convention of 1861, he and the other elected Walton County delegate argued for days against secession and war as a means of settling differences. The final vote was 7-2 and a dejected John Morrison did not attend the final assembly in Tallahassee. However, he was sent for and persuaded to sign the new Florida Constitution. Morrison's reluctant signature is the last on the document entitled "Ordinance of Secession."

Walton County paid a price for its opposition to slavery and secession. It became known as "Lincoln County", and, after the War, vigilantes from Mississippi and Alabama roamed the county looking for Union sympathizers. People were killed who were even rumored to have Union loyalty. Property was stolen; homes ransacked; mayhem was present for many months after the War ended in 1865.

A majority of Walton's men did join the Confederate Army after the war progressed and with the invasions of Union forces into Florida. They were outnumbered, and without the supplies of armaments, food and clothing available to Union soldiers. Their suffering in the cold of winters fighting in the mountains of Tennessee and in the long trek on foot to their homes in Florida when the war ended is barely acknowledged by historians.

This story is a fictionalized account of facts learned from stories heard in my youth. It is also based on research from archives in Florida, from official military records, and from records of the Presbyterian Church.

The physical setting in the Euchee Valley is as accurate as the writer recalls and affirmed by writers who wrote about their mid-1800 visits to Walton County. The personalities and activities of Archie and Billy Morrison were told to the writer by Aunt Jenny, the sister of Archie and Billy. The John Morrisons lived next door to the McCaskills and in close proximity to Knox Hill Academy; names of students at Knox Hill Academy in 1849-54 and 1867-68 are accurate; there were 25 African-American (slave) members among the predominantly Scottish members of the Euchee Valley Presbyterian Church prior to the Civil War.

The Story

The school year of 1854 was almost over for the children of Knox Hill Academy at Eucheeanna in Northwest Florida. The late April weather had suddenly turned warm after a long spell of rain. From his desk by a window of the schoolhouse, ten-year-old Archibald Morrison was day-dreaming. In his quiet way, Archie had observed that the surrounding woods looked greener and thicker than he ever recalled. The deer could hide better now, but so could the panthers. His father had cautioned him to be on the lookout for panthers, as they had been spotted by several reliable persons. Undeterred, Archie looked forward to the hike he planned to take on Saturday.

Streams would be flowing fast. Dogwood was in bloom, and if Elizabeth McLean went with him, they might pick violets. If Elizabeth wouldn't go with him, who should he ask? He wouldn't ask his cousin, Johnny McKinnon, because he was older and might make fun of stopping to pick flowers. When Mr. Newton had asked him to line up the children after recess, they had all followed Archie's directions and Elizabeth had smiled at him.

Suddenly, Mr. Newton's commanding voice intruded. "Children, you are all to memorize Bible verses 21-24, Chapter 5, in the Book of Amos, which concludes with 'Let justice roll down like waters and righteousness like an ever-flowing stream.' Younger children should ask an older brother or sister or your parents to help you. Children in grades 5 and 6 are to interpret and be prepared to discuss the meaning of the prophet's words." Pausing for emphasis, Mr. Newton had announced, "You are dismissed."

Knox Hill Academy students taking a break.

Now, Archie walked slowly down the path to his house. He was glad he lived close to the school and didn't have as long a walk as Johnny.

"Hey, Archie, wait for me." Without turning around, Archie knew it was Johnny McKinnon. Catching up with Archie, Johnny continued, "Did you hear about the meeting last night? The school trustees asked Mr. Newton to take the books about slavery from the shelves and Mr. Newton vowed he would not, saying, 'If the books go, I go.' What do you think he'll do?"

"I don't know," Archie answered crossly. "Papa was there, too, and I heard him tell my mother he wished Mr. Newton hadn't threatened to leave. But he also thinks the books shouldn't be carted off."

"Well, my father says those books just stir things up and people get riled and it's bad enough with that slavery story about *Uncle Tom's Cabin* getting folks all confused. How many farmers in Walton County to you think have slaves?"

"Besides your father? I don't know," replied Archie. "There's Lizzy. She was given to my mother by my grandfather when he died. My grandfather had the largest farmland around here needing lots of farm help. Lizzy was a slave, but she could leave if she wanted to, but she doesn't want to."

Johnny didn't answer but said, "I sure hope Mr. Newton doesn't leave. What would we do for a teacher if he left?"

"He lives here," Archie answered confidently. "Where would he go?"

Picking up the pace of his walk, Johnny, now running, shouted, "I don't know, but I gotta' run fast to help out at the mill. Papa told me to get there right after school was out because a big load of corn's coming in. See you tomorrow."

Behind him, he heard his younger brother, Billy, whistling that "Ring Around the Rosy" tune. That was Billy's way of teasing, of reminding Archie how he'd fallen down last week when Johnny jumped out at him from the bushes and playfully pushed Archie to the ground and then covered him with leaves. "Now you're dead and buried," Johnny had shouted. Billy couldn't believe that Archie hadn't tried to wrestle Johnny down. Instead, he just lay there, too embarrassed to get up with all the children gathered around.

Later, Archie would explain that he just felt funny, like he was supposed to wait for something and not get up. Billy never liked that explanation.

"Billy, cut out that whistling," Archie ordered. Billy's answer was to race off down the oak-lined road to the McCaskills' next door.

Sitting on the front porch steps, baby Angus in her arms, Archie's mother watched as Murdock and Malcolm, ages seven and five, chased each other round and round the yard. Spying Archie, the boys raced out to greet him.

Untangling himself from his brothers, Archie turned to his mother. "Mama, what did Papa and the other trustees decide last night about Mr. Newton and the books? And what's so wrong about the books anyway?"

"Archie, I'm sure the men know best what to do. However, I don't believe they reached a decision. Your father doesn't want Mr. Newton to leave and doesn't see how reading books about the main thing that's troubling the country can do any harm. After all, children like you need to know what people outside Florida are thinking."

Archie, still worrying, went into the house to change his clothes and attend to the chores he was expected to do. As he left, he called out, "I guess Billy's not coming to help me."

"Billy's gone to the McCaskills'," chanted Murdock, familiar with Billy's after-school visits to the neighbors.

"Boys," their mother ordered, "go see what you can do to help Archie." The younger boys obeyed, happy to feel they too could milk the cows and feed the fierce-looking but mild oxen.

Christian Morrison continued to sit on the steps, waiting for sight of her husband. She hadn't let on to Archie how worried she was about Mr. Newton and the books. As she and another wife of a school trustee had cleaned the church pews that morning, her friend had confided that her husband thought Mr. Newton was stirring up trouble and should be prevented from adversely influencing the children.

Christian hadn't agreed, but neither had she disagreed. She wanted to know exactly what Mr. Morrison thought.

John Morrison put in long days, but on this spring evening he would have daylight as he rode through the thick woods to his house. His job was co-owner and manager of a timber cutting business. Walton County was growing and lumber was needed for houses and businesses. Morrison also oversaw getting logs to Freeport on Choctawhatchee Bay. Oxen-drawn carts dragged the large pine logs from the woods to the sawmill. From there they were carried onto flat bed wagons and driven to the thriving port for loading onto barges. Delivery would be to other Southern towns where virgin heart pine was valued.

Christian soon gave up her watch for her husband and walked through the breezeway to the outdoor kitchen attached by a roof to the house. There Lizzy had begun warming the vegetables and ham left over from the midday meal.

Lizzy and Christian had known each other all their lives and enjoyed an easy, warm relationship.

"Christian," Lizzy began, "I heard you all talking about Mr. Newton. You knew, didn't you, that he's organizing a church just for us Negroes and is teachin' some of our children to read the Bible?"

Surprised, Christian replied, "No, Lizzy, I didn't know, but I think that's a nice idea, though I've always liked your being a member of the Euchee Valley Presbyterian Church."

John Morrison

"Well, I do, too, but there are those who don't like sittin' in the gallery and not really bein' part of the service. Mr. Newton says we can be a Presbyterian Church, too."

Before the two women could discuss this further, Billy burst into the kitchen and, with familiar enthusiasm, declared, "This supper smells so good I ran all the way home."

"Billy, please go help your brother and get the younger boys ready for supper."

"Mama," Billy complained, "why do I always have to take care of Murdock and Malcolm?"

"Because," Lizzy answered, "you have to do something around the place to help your mama, and 'sides, you're good at tendin' the boys."

The women enjoyed a shared laugh as Billy went out the door grumbling. Lizzy, who had no children of her own, was a second mother to Christian's fast-growing family. The Morrisons, thus far, had been fortunate that none of their children had been stricken with life-threatening illnesses so common at that time.

Now, as Christian and Lizzy began putting food on the table, the boys all rushed in. That is, all but Archie. Pensive and serious, Archie entered slowly with questions that had been bothering him.

"Mama, why did Papa differ with the others—like the trustees? And why will Mr. Newton leave?"

"Archie, we'll just have to wait until your father gets home to ask him about Mr. Newton. Remember your father doesn't always differ with others. But let's be glad someone is willing to try and have people consider all sides."

Afterword

What were the names of the books to which the trustees objected? According to McKinnon, "The books were entitled *Chambers Miscellanies*. They were very readable for young people—not deep. There was a vein of abolition running through them, but nothing at all like *Uncle Tom's Cabin*."

What happened to Mr. Newton and the books? Mr. Newton and the school trustees were all strong-willed Scotsmen. And, later, both the trustees and Mr. Newton had regrets about their swift action. After two years away from Eucheeanna (1854-56), he returned to teach in a new school building at Knox Hill Academy.

As it turned out, the trustees valued Mr. Newton, the teacher, more than insistence on determining the content of books. And, as time went on, the views of the abolitionist teacher were an influence on Walton County voters. They opposed secession from the United States of America and elected representatives to the 1861 Convention who voted according to the people of Walton County.

When war came to Northwest Florida, and with the sacrifices and upheaval of life for the Euchee Valley community, Mr. Newton became a target for criticism. With his wife and children, Mr. Newton made the arduous journey, via train and ship, from Northwest Florida to California, arriving in San Francisco. From there they traveled north to Healdsburg. Mr. Newton kept up a correspondence with friends in the Euchee Valley community, describing the beauty of Northern California an the moderate climate. But the family, especially his wife Margaret, was very homesick.

At the close of the War, the Newton family returned to Florida. Margaret died not too long after, never having fully recovered from the initial sea voyage and smallpox. Once again, Mr. Newton began to teach at Knox Hill Academy and to hold classes every Sunday for former slaves under a "brush arbor."

John Morrison and Alexander McCaskill were the elected delegates to the People's Convention (Secession Convention). To the end, they opposed secession but lost on a 62-7 vote.

Alexander McCaskill

Regardless of the benevolent treatment some

felt slaves received, the reality of the wrong inherent in one person's owning another became abhorrent to many in the religious community. According to John L. McKinnon's account, "The vote to oppose secession was almost unanimous."

What became of Archibald and Billy Morrison and John L. McKinnon? Although John Morrison, father of Archie and Billy, elected delegate to the Secession Convention of January, 1861, was a strong opponent of secession, when war ensued between the North and the South, both these sons joined the Confederate Army and were killed in the conflict.

An account of Lt. Archibald Morrison's death at the Battle of Nashville is given in McKinnon's *History of Walton County*. A synopsis of McKinnon's tragic discovery and burial of his cousin on the battlefield is included by Mark C. Curenton in *The Campbell Family*.

> "The Florida Brigade had taken up position of Shy's Hill near the west end of the main Confederate line south of Nashville in the early morning darkness of December 16. Morale was low. The men lacked proper clothing and shoes, and food was always scarce. Within the last three weeks the Confederate Army of Tennessee had been all but destroyed at the Battle of Franklin…
>
> Daylight on the morning of the 16th brought a federal artillery bombardment….At about 3:30 p.m., the brigade immediately to the Floridians' left was overwhelmed by a Union attach. Fearing capture themselves, the men from Florida threw down their rifles and fled in panic. Many of the men were captured, including Lt. John L. McKinnon. As he was being led away by his Yankee guards he heard a call from the woods. It was Archie Morrison. He had been wounded in the side by a stray bullet after he surrendered. Lt. McKinnon was permitted to stay with Lt. Morrison and comfort him. There, about dusk, with his head resting in Lt. McKinnon's lap, Archie Morrison died.
>
> John L. McKinnon spent the night digging a grave for Lt. Morrison. In the early morning hours of December 17, 1864, with the assistance of two Union soldiers, Archibald Morrison was laid to rest on the slope of Shy's Hill, just south of Nashville…"

William C. Morrison at age seventeen enlisted in Company K of the 6th Alabama Cavalry, a unit composed of men from Walton County. Family accounts state that Billy Morrison was killed in July, 1864, in an unsuccessful Confederate defense of a South Alabama railroad.

"HERE COME THE YANKEES"

Introduction

*I*n our quiet Southern town it was customary to visit relatives and friends on Sunday afternoons. We loved to visit great aunt Julia, especially because of Ellen's presence and her good stories.

Ellen was African-American and had lived all her life with Aunt Julia's family in Eucheeanna. When family members had all moved away or died, she went to DeFuniak Springs to live with Aunt Julia. Ellen lived to her ninety-fifth year.

In the early '30s, my father would regularly drive my mother, sister Chris and me thirteen miles into the country to Eucheeanna to visit our ancestral Presbyterian Church (founded in 1828) and the childhood home of his mother.

The house had been vacant for nearly ten years when I first saw it. We approached this large two-story frame house with awe, as my father began to tell us stories of its history. The barely visible remnants of fading white paint revealed that the life the house had once known was gone.

Ellen

Behind the house, one could see the foundations of the small houses once occupied by the domestic and farm workers, originally brought in as slaves. My great grandfather, Giles Bowers, had changed their status before the Emancipation Proclamation. However, most African-Americans remained right there until separated and scattered by the Civil War.

Now, this frail-looking, very old woman with very black skin was sitting with us and, at our request, preparing to tell us a story we'd heard many times but eagerly awaited. We sat in rocking chairs on Aunt Julia's small porch. Ellen's most dramatic story was "The Day the Yankees Come." Speaking in a soft voice, she became animated as she relived the events. Her speech was that of many African-Americans in the South in the 1860s. And, like some other ethnic groups translated and separated from their native languages, the letter "d" was used instead of "th" at the beginning of a word. Ellen began with "now here's de way it wuz the day de Yankees come".

Ellen's Story

"One mawnin' my mammy say a man come on a horse hollerin' dat de Yankees was comin'. He don' stop. He jus' keep goin' and hollerin'. Everybody scared nigh to death. Yore granpa say he don' know what's gon' happen."

"Granma quick as can be she ran and got de meal, just back from de mill, and sewed it up in an ol' mattress she figured no Yankee gon' want. Den, she took de good dishes and sunk 'em right down in de buckets we use to feed de pigs. She gave a handful of silver spoons to my mammy to quick-like hide in her house. Dat was all dey had time for. In no time a'tall here come de Yankees."

"'Fore you know it dey's all over de place. One big man, a cap'n or gen'ul, he walk about talkin' loud and big. He say dey gon' take over dis place. Den, he tell dem men what was with him to go to the fields and gather *everything*. Get all de cattle, and sheep and pigs and chickens. Don't leave nuthin'. Den, he say to other me to take Granpa and put him in de jail with de other white folks men who was left to take care of de women and chillum. All dem Yankees work fast, honey, and dey make our kind help 'em."

"One mawnin', dey ups and gits ready to leave. Dey bring Granpa from de jail and say dey gon' take him off to jail far away. My mammy say everybody begin to cry. Dey don' want Granpa to leave us. Lord, 'a mercy, honey, dem Yankees say to all our kind, 'Hitch up dem horses and de wagons and de buggies and git yoselfs ready. Y'all's gonna' go north too."

"De Yankees took everything cep'n scraps, but dey never find de meal or dishes or silver spoons what Granma and my mammy hid. Dey took all our kind cep'n de ones what was sickly an' ailin.' My mammy not well, so dey leaves me and my mammy an' de udder chillun."

While Ellen paused, remembering this troubling time, we waited quietly. Finally, I broke the spell.

"Ellen, Aunt Bern told us her grandmother, Granma, was very brave and didn't cry. She just walked up to the man in charge and asked him to please leave one horse so she could work the fields to provide food for the children."

"Dat's right. She did, but dat man don' pay her no mind. He jes' say bossy-like to dem mens, 'Do as I say, git goin'.' But another man what was standin' close by, he say quiet-like to de man holdin' ol' Vixen, 'Tie dat hoss to dat post and leave her.' Pore ol' Vixen 'bout ready to die anyway, but Granma glad to have her."

"Oh, honey, Granma she work and work so hard. How she manage nobody never knows. She took ol' Vixen and de half-grown chillun and she plow and hoe and work from dawn till late sundown. She allus the last to leave de field and den she help my mammy fix for us to eat. None of y'all can know what we all went through."

Ellen again lapsed into silence, staring off into the distance. My sister spoke up and asked, "Tell us about what happened when the War ended."

"Well, one day we hear dat ol' war was over. We knowed our folks not all gon' come back. Dey never could," Ellen added sadly, and I wondered if she was thinking of her own father. She signed and continued, "But Granpa he come back from dat ol' jail up North. I don' know how he done it, but he did."

"Ellen, didn't one of the men from Eucheeanna die in prison?" I asked.

"Oh, yes, honey, old Mr. Mac wut lived over the hill. Granpa say Mr. Mac died right dere beside him in dat jail, grievin' for his folks he had to leave here. I 'spect too dey never had enuff to eat cause Granpa looked mighty thin."

"Then what happened?" my sister asked.

"Well, Granpa and Granma went on workin'. Dey never rest. Dey work from 'fore day 'til no light left. Course, you know, dem crops never come up like before. Nothin' was like before, but dey manage."

"Pretty soon, dey send yore Aunt Lally off to school in Georgia. Lally say she gon' be a teacher and teach all us, white chillun and us, to read. And shore 'nuff, she did. Least she tried. Lally, she don' let *any* of de young 'uns in de valley quit. She say dey can read and she gon' make sure dey do.

Looking to us to emphasize the point, Ellen said, "Y'all remember, yore Aunt Lally was *somethin'*."

Ellen went on with her story. "When my mammy died, Granma puts me to sleep in a room right next to hers, an' I been close by ever since. Now it's yore Aunt Julia I tries to look after, but," Ellen stopped to laugh a small, cackling sound, "I guess you could say since Julia's young'n me she's takin' care of me. You see, I was dere, 'bout eight or nine years old when de Yankees come, but Julia weren't even born yet."

Turning to us, she said, "'Bout time y'all went home. I hear yore daddy sayin' good-bye to Julia and fixin' to leave."

"Yes, ma'am," I said as I reluctantly got up. "Good-bye, Ellen."

"Good-bye, child. Don' forget to say yore prayers."

"Yes'm, we will," my sister and I promised in unison.

Ellen had once again told the story to yet another generation of children. To her the events were as vivid as if they'd just occurred. To the listeners it would never be forgotten.

Footnote to "Yankees":

The Giles Bowers house in Eucheeanna was occupied by Union General Asboth as an encampment for his 700-man unit as they prepared for the attack on nearby Marianna. Their mission was (1) to release suspected Union Army prisoners in Marianna (*there were none to be found)*; (2) to recruit men for the Union Army (*erroneous rumor that Walton County had lots of Union sympathizers*); and (3) to collect slaves and transport them to the North.

The Union soldiers lived off the land and therefore the place was stripped of crops, animals and poultry. Upon the departure of the Army contingent, two women (and a dozen children) remained at the Bowers place.

The older men of Eucheeanna, who'd stayed in the community to look after women and children, were imprisoned in a tiny makeshift jail. When the Union soldiers departed Eucheeanna, the elderly men were taken away and jailed in prisons, some as far north as Elmira, New York. The men had committed no crimes. General Asboth simply felt they should not be allowed to remain.

This fact is documented in the Official Government Records of both Union and Confederate Armies in the War of the Rebellion.

Uniformed Federals on deck of gunboat Mendota, *bringing Parrot gun into position.*

Inside the Battery north of Fort McRee at Pensacola. Although the dress was not uniform, the weapons were always polished and ready. This is one of the batteries which later bombarded Fort Pickens and the Union fleet. It was held by the Confederates until May 2, 1862.

THE MUCH TRAVELED CONFEDERATE MONUMENT

Introduction

Many people don't realize Florida was one of the thirteen states of the "Old South" that joined the Confederacy. Others contest that fact with "but Floridians never fought in the Civil War. There were no battles there." Indeed, Floridians fought and died in the War Between the States. And there were two battles in Northwest Florida towns with skirmishes along the Union Army's march from Pensacola to Tallahassee and from Jacksonville inland. In the case of my county, Walton, the men joined when Union forces began to invade Northwest Florida.

Prior to that, Walton County was opposed to secession and war and so voted. The county then sent two delegates to the 1861 Secession Convention held in Tallahassee. One of the delegates was one of my great grandfathers, John Morrison. I have always treasured the heritage of Walton County's uniqueness during this historic time and the steadfast effort put forth in opposing secession from the United States of America. The final vote of the Convention delegates was 62 for secession and 7 opposed.

The most influential person in developing Walton County's position of opposition was the Reverend John Newton, an abolitionist, Amherst-educated, preacher/teacher imported to teach the children of the Scottish settlers. This charismatic man exerted unusual persuasive talent. That, combined with the moral opposition to slavery and war, convinced the deeply religious community of the rightness of its stand.

Ironically, John Morrison's two oldest sons were killed in the War that he had tried hard to prevent. And that last fact is a reason for the events associated with the Confederate Monument.

One of my earliest recollections of the story of the Confederate Monument in our town was overheard in whispered conversations. I heard it many times after that—on my grandmother Morrison's long veranda on a Sunday afternoon, when all the family gathered, and while visiting Great Aunt Julia sitting in rocking chairs on her smaller porch. And I heard it on Aunt Bern's patio again in whispered tones lest any passerby overhear the conversation. This time I recall being instructed, "Honey, we do not talk about this. It was long ago and the families have about gotten over it, now that the monument resides here in DeFuniak Springs."

What was so upsetting that an event which had occurred shortly after the conclusion of the Civil War in 1865 was recounted in whispered tones in the 1930s? And why did the tone of their voices go from a happy delight to one of quiet and secrecy? Here's the tale.

The Story

Shortly after the close of the Civil War, the women of Walton County pledged to raise money to have a memorial erected to honor those who lost their lives in the conflict. At first, with Florida under military rule, such a project was frowned upon as a statewide effort. Nonetheless, the women, empowered by their new roles during the War, would not be discouraged. Left alone to manage the farm, run the household and perform previously unaccustomed tasks, they felt nothing was impossible.

The organization soon broadened beyond Walton County and found supporters throughout the state. Letter writing and fund raising appeals were successful. With enough money—$250—available, they commissioned a sculptor in New Orleans to design an appropriate tribute to those who had sacrificed their lives. The mothers of young men lamented the fact that their sons would never realize their talents, never enjoy fulfillment of dreams and goals, never have families of their own. Surely some means of recognizing these sacrifices was important.

A report from a New Orleans sculptor who had been commissioned thrilled them with its description of the monument. It would be all marble, with a twenty-one inches square base; an obelisk column would rise to twelve feet capped by a human hand with the index finger pointing upward. There would be space enough to have carved the names of all the Walton County dead on its four sides.

Almost without discussion, the consensus was that it should be placed on the grounds of the Euchee Valley Presbyterian Church. The church had served for years as a community center. It now represented the stability and faith essential for the community to build life anew, not ever forgetting the young men of their county, now gone from their midst.

And so, when the great day came and the monument was delivered to the Euchee Valley Church, those close by came to marvel at the beautiful structure and to reminisce about the men whose names were listed.

Almost immediately, however, some of the community's leaders, all men, began to say that the monument really belonged on the courthouse grounds in Eucheeanna. Some of the ladies countered with the argument that the money raised had been given with the understanding that the tribute should be at the most revered placed in the county—the church. This was the oldest Presbyterian church in Florida and was the first public building erected by the early Scottish pioneers. The fallen soldiers deserved, they said, that their memories be honored in a more hallowed place than the courthouse.

Ultimately, the men who wished the monument moved to the Eucheeanna courthouse persuasively arranged with the president of the unincorporated, loosely organized group of ladies to have another vote taken. It was said, but never proven to the satisfaction of some, that the majority of those present voted to move the monument. There was also the argument that some of the ladies, who wanted the monument to remain in the churchyard, were not informed of the meeting.

There was further speculation that John L. McKinnon, the owner of forty-five slaves and against the County's anti-secession position, had resented Morrison's representation of the County at the Secession Convention. And that the McKinnon family had exerted its influence over the vote of the ladies' organization. However, the monument was moved to the courthouse grounds.

John Morrison, serious, deliberative delegate to several Florida Constitutional Conventions, vowed to stop this move. He had lost two sons and a nephew in the War and felt betrayed at the last minute change of plans for the monument's placement. He had also contributed generously to its creation, though this was never revealed.

With his son, Murdock, and their employees, they very quietly arranged to return the monument to the churchyard. This clandestine maneuver was accomplished by working into the night, taking care not to harm the beautiful marble memorial. With dawn approaching, the monument was loaded onto the dray and cautiously carried back to its original home.

With the morning discovery of the missing monument, alarm was sounded—until someone happened by the churchyard and saw the obelisk boldly commanding attention from its original location.

Those who had engineered the monument's move to the courthouse furiously and verbally attacked the rumored perpetrators of the midnight deed. The president of the women's group, with the encouragement of D. L. McKinnon, sued the accused Morrisons. The judge of the circuit court ruled in favor of the defendants, claiming there was no proof of damages, as charged, or of the rumored threats of violence…Further, there had never been proof of a majority vote to change the placement of the monument from churchyard to courthouse. The case was dismissed.

Not satisfied with the ruling, the leader of the women's group, again with attorney McKinnon's services, appealed to the Supreme Court of Florida. There the ruling was in favor of the organization, even though no referee was assigned to inquire into the facts of the matter, nor were there minutes from the meetings of the unincorporated group of women. The monument, nonetheless, was ordered returned to the Eucheeanna courthouse.

Again, the monument made the journey from churchyard to courthouse. Families took sides, arguments continued. Even in church children learned, without being taught, whom to speak to and whom to avoid. It would take generations to recover the unity of spirit once felt by the Scottish pioneers.

Today, the much-traveled monument stands peacefully on a slight knoll of the courthouse grounds in DeFuniak Springs, the current county seat. One face of the monument says: "To the memory of the Confederate dead of Walton County, Florida." The names of the 91 men who lost their lives are inscribed on two sides of the marble obelisk. This was the first monument in Florida dedicated to the memory of the Confederate dead.

The Walton County Court House, DeFuniak Springs, Florida, with the Confederate monument in the foreground.

THE MYSTERIOUS DEATH OF UNCLE JOHN

Introduction

As a child growing up in DeFuniak Springs, Florida, in the 1930s, I repeatedly heard the story of my father's brother, Jim, running home from the L & N Railroad Station waving a copy of the message he had picked up while learning the Morse Code and use of "the wires." Tears streaming down his face, he rushed into the house, located only a few blocks from the station, with the terrible news that his older brother John had died in Poughkeepsie, New York. The year was 1900.

That image of the trauma of this event was revisited over and over by my father's family, usually when they met to talk on my grandmother Morrison's veranda. The shocking news of the death of the nineteen-year-old son the parents had sent off to school in New York upset the family for many years. Uncle John, they said, was very smart. The family expected he would go into the banking business his father planned for Northwest Florida. Grandfather Malcolm Morrison was instrumental in starting a bank in DeFuniak Springs, but his ambition for his sons ended with the death of his eldest son.

I heard many versions of the cause of the death of Uncle John, because the original message in the telegram from a school administrator gave no specific cause. I heard speculation quoting someone who visited the school, another offered by one of the young men from DeFuniak who also attended the school. One version was that John had been the victim of a gas leak. Another believed he had typhoid fever. Yet another believed there had been a faulty plumbing system.

In September 1994 I began correspondence with the Poughkeepsie Reference Librarian. That turned into an unusual inquiry piqued by the interest of the librarian. Together with the letters John wrote to his siblings, much history of the era is revealed: education, the cover-up conducted by the school and its founder, Harvey Eastman, the conditions of public health, and the interests of John himself. Most of all, I finally learned the exact cause of death and why for all those years there was confusion about it.

The Story

Gathering in front yards in homes all around the Lake, people were talking about the mysterious death of John Morrison, son of Malcolm and Chrissie Morrison, who had moved to DeFuniak Springs only a few months earlier. People in town knew the Morrisons. Malcolm and Chrissie had originally lived in the Euchee Valley, first home in Florida of the many Scots who had emigrated to Northwest Florida from North Carolina in the early 19th century, and before that from the Isle of Skye, Scotland. After their marriage, they had moved to the village of Argyle, located near the new town of DeFuniak Springs.

Malcolm's father had been one of the two delegates to what became known as the Secession Convention of 1861. In that position he had represented the predominant feeling of the County that they did not want secession from the United States of America, and they were opposed to the continuance of slavery. Mr. John Morrison, the former delegate and later representative in the legislature, was highly respected in politics and as a businessman dealing in large acreage of timber and lumber mills. People always said it was ironic that, although he had personally and as a representative of Walton County opposed secession and war, his two oldest sons joined the Confederate army when Union forces invaded North Florida and were killed in the war.

My grandfather, Malcolm, who was just a child when the War Between the States ensued, as an adult was the one to manage the Morrison lumber business. He also had plans for starting a bank in the County's fastest growing town, DeFuniak Springs. The town with the pretty little lake had been selected by railroad executives when the L & N railroad was routed close by the lake as a potential winter resort. The railroad would bring Northern visitors if there were some major attraction in addition to the beauty of the place and the climate. The idea of the town's becoming the Southern counterpart of the Chautauqua in upstate New York took hold, and the town did flourish in this context.

The family of Malcolm M. and Chrissie Bowers Morrison, circa 1893.
Children, left to right: (seated) Malcolm A. Morrison, Kate Douglass Morrison, (standing)
Bernice Bowers Morrison , John M. Morrison, James Bowers Morrison.

It was important that the sons of Malcolm and Chrissie, John and his younger brothers, Jim and Malcolm, know the advantages of the education they would receive in DeFuniak rather than the village of Argyle. They had built a house with a view of the lake, enrolled the children in school, and begun to take an active part in the Presbyterian Church, when it was decided that John should go to a New York school touted in banking circles as the best institution to train future bankers. Harvey Eastman had founded the Eastman School of Business in a southern New York city, Poughkeepsie on the Hudson River, which focused on banking as a profession.

Late at night Chrissie and Malcolm could be heard by the children discussing the possibility of John's going off to this school. Malcolm argued for it, even promising to involve friends of John's and their parents in the idea. They could use several smart young businessmen in this fast growing part of the South. Chrissie did not like her son being so far away from home. By train it would take two, perhaps three, days to go from DeFuniak to Poughkeepsie, and the cost was not small, so John could not come home often. Why couldn't he just attend the local vocational school, which had a good reputation? No, was the answer, he must have the best, most advanced education and training in banking. John must be properly prepared to lead that challenge. Already, he had excelled in local schools.

After the agreement of Chrissie's nephew, Bowers Campbell, also to go to Poughkeepsie, plans for John to leave in time for the summer session took over. There were trips to Pensacola on the train to purchase adequate clothing for the more chilly New York climate. John began to read about New York City with real excitement at all the plays and concerts and sporting events he might see. All around was excitement as the day of departure arrived.

Relatives of the families gathered at the train station to send the boys off with all their good wishes. Chrissie had also packed a box of fried chicken, potato salad, biscuits with haw jelly for the first day's journey. She did this although her husband protested that there would be a dining car on the train and John could and should experience this. The mother had checked and double-checked her son's suitcase to make sure he had packed the winter underwear they had ordered from Sears, Roebuck & Co. John said he would never wear those ugly, sticky things, but Chrissie insisted he take them along, just in case.

"Watch out for cinders, Mother," her husband warned. Chrissie was not wiping cinders from her eyes, but tears. Her beloved oldest son had never spent a single night away from home and now he was going hundreds of miles away. John's reply had been, "Well, Mama, it isn't as far as Harvard College and likely isn't as cold."

"Maybe you'll learn to ice skate like *Hans Brinker and the Silver Skates*," brother Jim added. "And John, what about seeing prize fights in Madison Square Garden? Will you get to do that?"

The DeFuniak Springs railroad station

"I doubt it, Jim. The fights are at night and I think students have to be in by nine o'clock."

"We'll sure miss you on the baseball team, John," said a friend who had come to say good-bye.

"I know, Ernest, I'll miss you and the team too. Maybe I'll get to see a World Series game in New York."

"Here it comes down the track," shouted young Malcolm. "John, John, it's comin' straight at you. Move back so you won't get hit," the worried younger brother exclaimed. The older boys laughed at this concern and lack of knowledge about trains and tracks.

John turned to his family. "Good-bye, Mama," John said as he kissed her cheek. "Don't cry. I'll be back before you know it." His mother could not speak as she clutched his arm while he moved towards his father.

"Good-bye, Papa. I'll try to make you proud of me."

"Why, John," his father said, "I'm already proud of you. Take good care of yourself in that northern clime."

"Yes, sir, I will," John promised.

Sisters Kate and Bernice were next in line. Kate, the younger, was crying and begged, "Don't go, John. Please don't leave us."

"I have to go to school, sweet Kate, but I will write you and we'll have such a good time talking about it all when I get home."

"Now, Bern, I hear there's a real catch in the Gillis clan. He's presently in school in Boston, but upon his return he plans to move to DeFuniak Springs."

Bernice came back quickly. "John, I have absolutely no interest whatsoever in these boys you keep telling me about or bringing home. I will miss you but not your efforts to have me meet more boys. Good-bye and do write to us."

"Oh, I'll write, but you must write me the news of any new folks who move here with pretty girls. Hey, Bern, maybe she'll have a brother you'll like."

It looked for a minute as if Bernice would swing at her brother, but she thought better of it in such a crowd of well-wishers as had gathered.

Jim and Malcolm were next, with Jim teasing, "You know, John, our sister, Bernice, is likely the only seventeen-year-old spinster in DeFuniak Springs."

"Watch out, Jim. Bernice will get even with you for that."

"John," his father called, "the conductor is motioning for you to get on board."

"Yes, sir, I see him," John replied.

"Well, Malcolm, I have to run. Work hard to beat those Campbell kids in school."

"I will, John," Malcolm called after his brother, who by now was on the steps leading into the sleeping car.

"Good-bye," everyone present chorused as they waved and waved till the train was out of sight.

John's trip was apparently uneventful. He boarded the L & N Railroad line in the early evening, went through Pensacola and onto the nearby town of Flomaton, Alabama, where he had to change trains. From there he went north to Chicago, changing trains once more for the final stretch to New York. He wrote home about getting settled, what the school was like, and something of the makeup of the school's students.

The following are letters written to his sisters, Kate and Bernice, and to his brother, Jim.

5 Lent Street

Poughkeepsie, 7/26/1900

My dear Kate,

Bernice need not make fun of your letters for they are just as nice as can be. I love to get a letter from you. How I wish you were here to sit in my lap. I almost cry when I think that I would not let you when I was at home. I would love to write more but I really don't have the time, but don't you forget to write to me.

This school gets harder every day. May be we will finish by Christmas or may be it will be a whole year, but whether I finish or not I won't stay here but three months. Uncle Daniel wrote Bowers that Ben was going to leave Tuesday, so he ought to get here tomorrow morning. When you go home be sure and mail me a letter or two letters on the way, so I will know how you got through. The little peaches at our window are getting pretty ripe. It rained here all last night and part of the day. Does Bernice hear from Ed Watson?

Don't I wish I was in DeFuniak now so I could be with Miss Singleton.

I like to get to read Flora Belle's letter and Abbie's, too. Does Mamma improve any?

Whenever I send Bernice music, I will send you some too. I had a letter from Mary G. Morrison today and one from Annie the other day, but have not had time to answer. We are both well but I am awful tired.

Your loving brother,
John

5 Lent Street

Poughkeepsie, NY, Aug.

Dear Bernice,

I have received two or three letters from you in the last few days but haven't had the time to answer. I don't remember getting one addressed to Jno Murphy Morrison. Maybe I got it but didn't notice. I will look through my trunks for it. If I find it I will address your next one to suit you.

Tell mamma I am getting over my homesick spell, but if things are hard again at school to-morrow it will come on me again.

We had lots of fun today about the beef. It was the toughest thing I ever saw. Every one of us had something to say about it. I don't like anything they have to eat but get along alright, it is so funny to me. Every time we go to the table Edwin starts up something to laugh at.

We have a new boarder here from Tallahassee, Fla. He is brother to the State Treasurer Whitfield. He entered school last Thursday. There are now ten Florida boys at this school... Every state in the Union is represented, and there are students from China, Japan, and Cuba. One of our teachers teaches the English language to the foreign students. The little Japs are the brightest, quietest, and funniest boys here. Tell mamma I just have to write on Sunday but I don't study. We go to preaching twice on Sundays. If you would just come off as far as I have to school you would be glad to go to school at DeFuniak. When I get home I will crow and talk big about not having to go to school.

6 Vassar Street
Po'keepsie, NY, Sept. 3

Dear Jim,

Well, Jim I went out about two miles to see a baseball game this evening, between Poughkeepsie and Kingston and it was a rocky game. I had rather see DeF play any time. Kingston has a fairly good team and beat the other 13 to 6. Edwin is the funniest boy and he gets out on the street and cuts up and then gets nearly scared to death because he thinks the policeman is after him. How are you and Blox getting along with the wires? When I go home I will know how to keep any sort of books. You ought to see Prof. McDonald make the boys hustle at school. He almost jumps on some of them. We are all going to the opera tonight. I think it will be good. Our new boarding place has good fare and it is so much cooler. How is Gillis and the girls? From what I can hear he must be the only beau in Argyle. Does he make anything stacking lumber? What is Earnest Edge doing now? You all were writing a while back about Earnest being there—was it Earnest Edge? Well, Jim, the "Kid" couldn't touch Corbett. I hear Fitz is going out of the ring. I believe if he would try he would be the champion again. What do you think about? No more news up here. Write me the Argyle dots.

Your brother,
John

John was not to know many more days at the Eastman School of Business for he became very ill. When he died, the death was unanticipated, at least by the school administration. The notice of John's death to his parents was matter of fact, without mentioning the cause of death. That led to the decades of questions about his death.

Attached are copies and excerpts of letters from the Eastman School that Chrissie kept and pondered. Her comment upon resurrecting this sad time was, "I'm not certain how John died. Why didn't the school notify us that he was gravely ill?"

That semi-indictment would then be swept away with comments about how lovely the young ladies from Vassar were to write, to continue to write to her. "Oh, yes," Baba would say, "telegrams, letters and even flowers for the funeral. Your grandfather attended to all the arrangements, not getting enough sleep or eating right. The other sad fact is that he became ill and we had to let others take care of him. I didn't think I could get through the separation and worry, but somehow I managed." Looking at those family members gathered she'd say, "How good of you all to keep me company."

Someone always asked, "But what was the final answer as to what caused the death of Uncle John?" "My dear," Baba would reply, "we just do not know."

And thus was planted in my head the determination to find out one day the cause of the death of the Uncle John I never knew.

Minimal information about John's death from the Eastman School left the family grief stricken and mystified.

A message arrived at the DeFuniak Springs L & N Railroad station, via the wireless, saying approximately the following:

November 3, 1900

Please notify Mr. and Mrs. Malcolm Morrison of the death of their son, John, at the Business School in Poughkeepsie, New York. When more facts are known, the school will be in touch with the family.

Eastman School of Business
Poughkeepsie, N.Y.

November 3, 1900

Dear Mr. and Mrs. Morrison:

It is with deep regret that I inform you of the death of your son, John. Just a few days ago, I saw John merrily walking with a group of students on their way to get the train to New York City bound for the Metropolitan Opera House.

The cause of his death is not presently known to us. Upon his roommate's noting John's distress, he called to the house manager, who called the local physician who had been tending John for several days. A very high temperature was recorded. The Dr. stayed with John for most of the night. By early morning your son left this earth planet. As members of the Christian faith, we know he now rests in a glorious place.

I believe you know his roommate, Bowers Campbell, who may be your nephew. Bowers is as puzzled by the illness as we are. He is in good health, so we have ruled out a possible gas leak. The high temperature suggests some infectious disease, but we just cannot trace any cause. If and when the cause of death is established, we will inform you, of course. There will be a delay in return of the body until the cause of death is determined.

Meanwhile, please accept my sympathy for I know the loss of your son is tragic. I understand the young ladies of Vassar College have heard of John's death and plan to contact you. He was a very popular young man with such gracious manners and excellent deportment.

Meanwhile, please let us know how we can accommodate your plans in any way.

Yours sincerely,
John McDonald

The Poughkeepsie Reference Librarian entered into the research in 1994. The librarian discovered a very brief obituary in the local newspaper of November 1900. She speculated that Mr. Eastman would not have wanted any publicity about a death from typhoid fever at his school. Yet there were numerous deaths from the dread disease at the turn of the century in New York State and in Poughkeepsie until 1937.

I was advised to seek a death certificate from the New York Bureau of Vital Statistics. I did, and it arrived several months later, verifying the cause of death as typhoid. At last, there was certainty to explain why a healthy young man died so suddenly (though it turns out he was tended for a high fever for several days prior to dying).

The librarian speculated that John might have gone off the school premises and drunk contaminated water. Or the water at the school might have been contaminated, but with only a few students affected at the time of John's illness and death.

In 1900 there were 51 cases of typhoid fever reported and 11 deaths from the disease in Poughkeepsie. In 1907 there were 168 cases reported with 30 deaths. In 1937 there were five persons with one death. Because of the knowledge about the need for pure drinking water, there were no further cases reported in Poughkeepsie in the succeeding years.

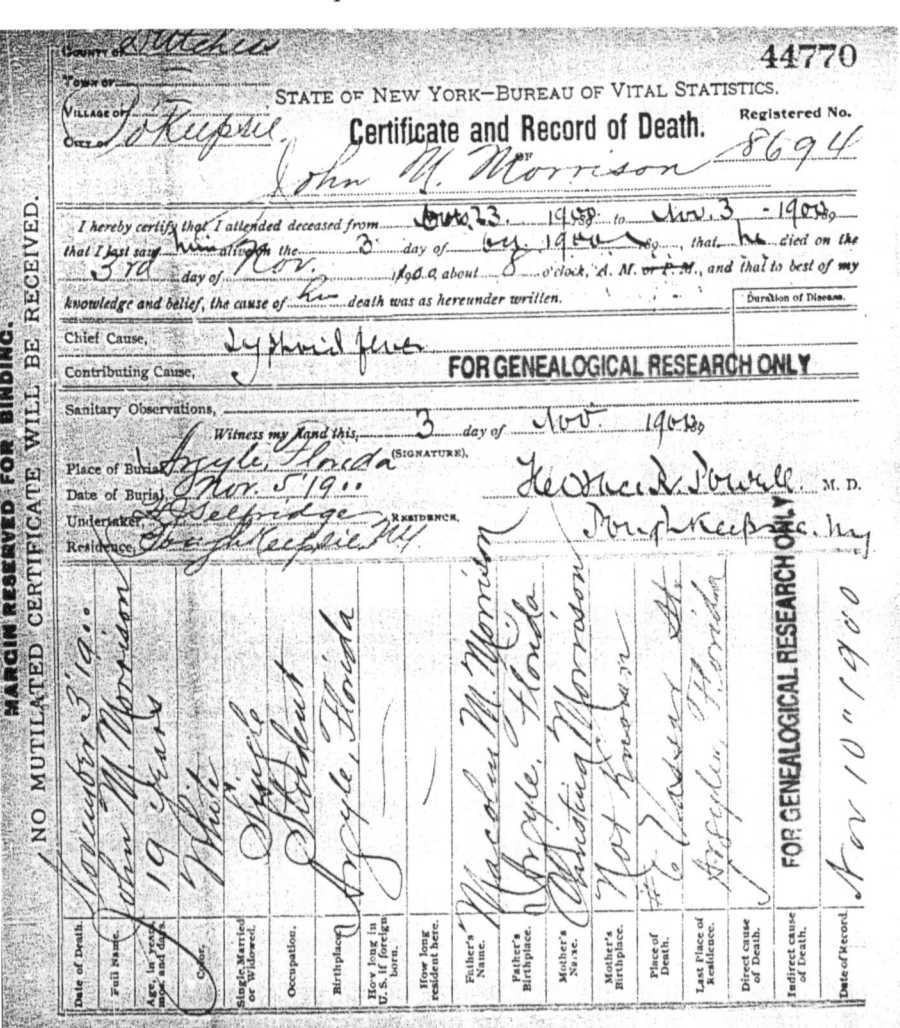

John Morrison's death certificate

THE SUNDAY AFTERNOON CONTEST

Introduction

On a quiet Sunday afternoon in the early 1930s, a frequent activity in our Northwest Florida town was our Aunt Bern's instructional as well as entertaining contest on the Bible. This would follow midday dinner at Grandmother Morrison's house. Aunt Bern would call together her daughter Kay, our friend Frances, my sister Chris and me to meet her on the side veranda which had a lovely view of the lake.

Always we watched the lake when seated in the large rocking chairs on the veranda.

Aunt Bern home from church

On this warm Sunday afternoon there was more to see than the sunshine glistening on the lake. A rowboat and a sailboat were a strange sight on a Sunday afternoon. They were occupied by men who appeared to know one another, as their voices and laughter carried up the hill to the veranda.

What captivated our attention was the effort by those in the sailboat. There was no wind at all. It was a very hot July afternoon. In addition, neither swimming nor boating was allowed on Sundays. The scene before us caused us to forget the reason we were sitting there waiting for Aunt Bern.

For a while I thought they might be drunk like the comedians we saw in the movies. They were making so much noise it just didn't seem real. Suddenly, Aunt Bern appeared. "What on earth are those men doing in boats on the lake on Sunday? I'll have to call the sheriff. Girls, take out your Bibles and study the Ten Commandments while I telephone the sheriff."

If Aunt Bern chose to quiz us on the Ten Commandments, I was ready.

The Story

I grew up in an area of the country categorized today as "the Bible Belt". However, I don't recall anyone ever taking verses out of context to prove a point. The Ten Commandments, on the other hand, were specific and to be honored.

In Sunday school, at home or visiting relatives, the children were asked to recite the Ten Commandments. I knew them well with little understanding of most. Some I did puzzle over but rarely questioned. The seventh commandment I particularly avoided asking about for fear, from the adults' voices, that it was as bad a thing as having ancestors.

Uncle Ira, Mamma's brother, caused me worry and reduced my sister to tears when he solemnly and with alarm asked, "Did you know you had ancestors?" From his tone of voice, we knew it was a bad thing to have and I was afraid committing adultery was just as bad.

It was easy to understand "Thou shalt not kill or steal" (the sixth and eighth commandments). And I knew from punishment I'd received that "Thou shalt not take the name of the Lord thy God in vain (the third commandment) was very wrong. I had picked up the slang expressing "Gosh", repeated it in my father's presence without any recognition that "gosh" was a substitute for God. In reflection, I think, my father, not a stern man or harsh disciplinarian, was especially concerned that his children not use slang.

Chris and Marjorie Morrison

Trying to keep the Sabbath day holy (the fourth commandment) was a very familiar commandment in my family and for most of our associates. As long as my grandmother lived, the swings were tied up, the funny papers put away until Monday, and the midday meal, which we always had at Baba's, had been prepared the day before and only needed "warming up". I wonder now how "warming up" was more sacred than actual cooking.

The fifth commandment was repeated often, though we had no reason not to honor our parents. It may be, however, that the unconscious absorption of this commandment kept me from committing sins when away at college. Sins like attending a movie on Sunday, smoking, or sitting in a parked car at night with a boy just never occurred to me to challenge. They were unspoken rules I followed.

Let me add that I don't think I was ever self-righteous or critical of other girls. After all, they had come from South Florida, a pretty godless place, or so Daddy had said when, after a visit there, we told him of our shock that the stores were open on Sundays. In our town, stores were closed on Sundays. He responded, "Well, those people love money so I guess on Sundays they go to stores as their place of worship."

The ninth commandment, "Thou shalt not bear false witness against your neighbor"—what was that? I never asked these questions since I thought as the older sister I should know. Of course, I didn't want to show my ignorance. Mamma patiently explained that one must not talk about one's neighbors in a critical way. I wondered if that included what I'd heard Daddy say about our new neighbors.

I did not covet anything about our new neighbors, so that commandment was easy (the tenth commandment). But what was a "graven image" (the second commandment) that thou should not have? The answer by Sunday school teacher gave was that we should not have idols—only worship God (the first commandment). What were idols, I wondered, but didn't ask. Years later, when movie idols became a much-used description, it occurred to me that Miss Mary Smith was substituting Nelson Eddy, who she said was her idol, for God.

You might think I grew up in a strict, conservative home in conduct and politics. To be sure, manners and behavior were conservative by today's standards. But in politics my father was an outspoken Democrat. Today he would be called a "liberal," for his frequent and steady reference during those Depression years to the need for the government to "do something about the poor" and his disdain for "calling up the military at every turn." As to the label of liberal, I think he would deny that and answer that he was only following his religion.

Like his sister Bernice, and the other Scottish Presbyterians of their community, they were well versed in the Bible. And Aunt Bern was determined the children in her family would also know this source of information and guidance.

While Aunt Bern had been calling the sheriff, my sister wandered over to the swings and was looking longingly at them. She knew not to get on one and swing as this was the Sabbath. Kay and Frances had begun to discuss the boys in their class and their relative merits. And I had been occupied thinking of the Ten Commandments. I planned to win this contest.

Aunt Bern reappeared, and with her usual enthusiasm, said, "Come on, girls, it's time to see who knows the most answers to questions about the Bible."

There were no prizes, but each of us hoped to be the first to answer. "All right," Aunt Bern would begin, "who can name all the books of the Old Testament?"

In unison we would all begin confidently. "Genesis, Exodus, Leviticus, Numbers, Deuteronomy." The older girls made it to the end, while Chris and I watched their lips and echoed their recitations.

"Aunt Bern," I asked, "aren't we going to talk about the Ten Commandments?"

"Well, honey, since we did that a few weeks ago and you knew them so well, I thought today we'd think about other parts, other stories, in the Bible. Now, where was Jonah headed when he was swallowed by the whale?"

Frances Lathinghouse, Grandmother Morrison (Baba), and Kay Stuart Gillis

"Was he going fishing?" I ventured. Aunt Bern shook her head.

"I think he was going to Nineveh," said Frances quietly.

"That's right, Frances. Marjy and Chris, you will know this one. Who was Abraham's son?"

"Isaac," my sister and I shouted, happy to get the spotlight.

"Was he Abraham's only and first-born son?"

"Yes, yes," we proudly proclaimed.

"Well," Aunt Bern replied thoughtfully, "maybe not. Someone look up Genesis 16, verse 15 and tell us."

Kay, accustomed to her mother's technique of always looking things up, jumped up to consult the Bible and said, "No, Abraham's first son was Ishmael. But," Kay continued, "I thought Sarah was Abraham's wife and they were old when Isaac was born, so where did Ishmael come from?"

My father had quietly joined us on the porch and, with a teasing voice, said to his sister, "Yes, Bernice, explain that, please. Did old Abraham have two wives at the same time?"

Aunt Bern ignored this and moved on, saying, "All you have to remember is that Abraham had two sons."

"But what happened to Ishmael?" my sister asked. Since Ishmael was new to us, we were curious about him.

"Well, honey, he and his mother were told to leave and were sent out into the desert."

I thought my tender-hearted sister would cry as, with her vivid imagination, she pictured this in her mind.

"Did they die out there?" she whispered.

"No, they didn't, honey. Later I'll tell you more. For now you can remember that Isaac became head of the tribes of Israel and Ishmael became head of the Arab people."

Aunt moved on. "Who led the Israelites out of bondage in Egypt?"

This was before Cecil B. DeMille and the Biblical movies, so we knew it was Moses, not Charleton Heston.

"Who were God's chosen people?"

Before any of us girls could answer, my father, still sitting just behind us spoke up and emphatically stated, "The people of DeFuniak Springs, Florida!"

"Malcolm," Aunt Bern said, "do stop confusing the children."

"Well, Bernice, it's sometimes confusing to me. What do you think, girls," Daddy continued, "was the whole world created in six days?"

"Yes, yes."

"Ah, well," Daddy said, "I wonder, don't you?"

"And Daddy says the Garden of Eden was in Geneva, Alabama, where Mamma grew up," I added. "Because Mamma thinks Geneva is Paradise."

"Well, my dear, your Daddy likes to tease," Aunt Bern replied. That ended the Bible contest. "Now, let's all go have a piece of caramel cake."

As Aunt Bern walked with quick, purposeful steps past my father, I heard him say, "Next week, Bernice, I'd like to hear you explain predestination."

"Malcolm, you are the limit! You know as much about predestination as I do. Come on and have a piece of cake."

My father's tone turned serious as he continued to talk while we trailed behind him and Aunt Bern towards the breakfast room where the luscious cake was waiting.

"Frankly," he said, "I wish our Presbyterian brethren would give up that doctrine. To me, it simply allows the comfortable, the well-off folks to forget the poor people. The rich somehow think God favors them and they deserve good fortune. I just don't believe it's all predestined. However," he said with a smile, "I do believe I am destined to have a piece of caramel cake with these lovely young ladies."

With that, the four girls giggled and sat down to enjoy the cake. "Praise God from whom all blessings flow," my father intoned as he tasted the first bite of cake.

"Amen," was the happy response from my Methodist-influenced sister and me.

AUNT BERN'S LEGENDARY PARTIES

Introduction

*I*t was widely acknowledged in my hometown that my Aunt Bernice gave the best parties in town. Invitations to a luncheon, tea or dinner were treasured as were evening parties for her daughter and nieces.

Holiday dinners and special occasions to which the whole family was invited were also sparkling, happy times. The same attention to good food, lovely table decoration and service was present for family or guests.

Aunt Bern's menus at all dinners featured simple, but extraordinarily delicious fare. Chicken, roast beef, turkey and ham were always cooked to perfection. Vegetables had no exotic sauces, nor were they overcooked as in so many Southern households. Desserts were elegant and luscious. Aunt Bern enjoyed baking and no one would ever forget her several-layered Lady Baltimore cake with raisins, nuts, and coconut filling midst white icing, or the rich and smooth Devil's Food cake or beautiful parfaits of fruit with ice cream or whipped cream made unique by her creativity. Hot breads so essential to every Southern meal were unfailingly perfect. Rolls were Aunt Bern's specialty. Biscuits and cornbread were Rebecca's.

Rebecca, the cook, had been working for Aunt Bern for many years and the understanding between them usually didn't require much verbal communication. They each knew the other's strengths and desires for good food and worked to fulfill that. The classic remark I recall from Rebecca was when I questioned the amount of canapés and little cakes prepared for a tea. Rebecca looked at me in disbelief. "Honey, it's like to told your Aunt Bernice. If you can't do it right, don't do it a'tall. And it's better to have too much than not enough."

Aunt Bern's Advice

I sought advice about party-giving from Aunt Bern many times as we sat on our porch or next door on Aunt Bern's patio. As friends passed by on walks around the lake, or driving in cars, we waved or called out greetings--a slight distraction, but necessary to maintain connection with the long-time friends.

"Now, honey," Aunt Bern, my father's sister, instructed when asked for advice, "the important thing to remember about any party is the people. If you fuss with too fancy food or flower arrangements or polishing silver until you're worn out, your party will flop. You have to be in charge and ensure that your guests have a good time. The minute the door bell rings with one guest or one hundred, throw open the door, greet them with a big smile and pretend you've just been waiting around doing nothing—waiting for them, though you've likely been preparing for days."

"The next thing," she continued, "is being ready. Nothing so distracts a hostess as thinking of all the things she hasn't finished. Of course, last minute trials do occur, like plumbing problems, but you can turn that into a funny story, if you don't over-do it."

Kay Stuart Gillis and her mother, Bernice Morrison Gillis.

Being prepared was essential. I'd long observed planning sessions between my mother and aunt with pencils and paper in hand. Aunt Bern organized every detail of any party. There was nothing she overlooked or left to chance.

Implicit in Aunt Bern's directions to the younger members of the family were instructions on manners. Once when I began to tell of a visit to the dentist, Aunt Bern said, "My dear, we do not discuss dental work at the table."

Another time, when out shopping for ingredients for a special party, I walked towards a water fountain, and Aunt Bern quickly stopped me. "Honey," she said, "horses drink from troughs, not people."

The most often repeated story about Aunt Bern's dinners was one I heard many times on conversational early evenings on our porch or heard someone else repeat it as if new. This is the story about my father's refusal to attend a dinner party in honor of the governor.

Dinner with the Governor

There is one story that made the rounds of what's usually characterized as "gossip" but is considered acceptable conversation in a small town. This was about my father's refusal to attend a dinner party with the governor. Mostly the following is accurate as I recall but slightly embellished as I too listened to the tale told on porches in the summertime. However, I had the advantage of first hearing this discussed by my parents as I lay in bed in the next room. The conversation between them went something like this:

"But Malcolm, what will your sister think if we don't attend? This is a very special occasion."

"Bernice knows how I feel about this no-good fellow. I've made it perfectly clear in the past that I have absolutely no respect for the man. I wouldn't sit at the same table with him for a million dollars."

"But what about Stuart? This is important to him, you know."

"How Stuart can stand this absolutely without merit man, much less be cordial to him, is beyond me."

"Malcolm, Bernice has spent a great deal of time in planning and preparation for this party. I think you should consider what it means to both of them."

"If Stuart thinks he can somehow imbue the governor with high standards, there's not enough time in the world to do so, and besides, the man is not good material for improvement."

"I wish you would not outright refuse. Think about it, please."

"Please do not bring this up again. I will explain to Bernice. Stuart may not like for a while, but he'll get over it. It's settled. We are not going."

I recall feeling sorry for Mamma because this was a big event. My aunt entertained beautifully, whether in her home in DeFuniak Springs or in Tallahassee, the state capital, when Uncle Stuart served as president of the State Senate. I knew my mother would like to attend. Most of all, she did not want strained feelings in the family.

The root of my father's antipathy towards the governor lay in Daddy's having served in the Navy with him during World War I. The governor apparently had used his higher rank in ways my father considered autocratic and demeaning to others. My father could not abide people who used authority to intimidate. At the dinner table we would regularly hear critical accounts of persons he considered too filled with their own importance. It's fortunate he was in business for himself, as he did not like taking orders from anyone. The whole military experience, therefore, was anathema to him. And towards this man in particular he had unrelenting feelings of animosity and distrust.

Redeeming humor, however, resulted from the dinner party. It seems that when Rebecca, the cook whose biscuits were famous for their melt-in-the-mouth quality, was serving to the governor, he turned to her and, in a syrupy, patronizing way, said, "Rebecca, these biscuits are so good. I'll bet you don't know how many I've eaten." "Yes, sir, I do," emphatically replied Rebecca, "that makes ten."

The governor, of course, did not know that Rebecca was never, ever obsequious and that even a hint of condescension, though passing as praise, brought a strong response. She was ever her own person. The governor, we were told, saved the situation by leading the laughter. "Rebecca, you're an honest woman."

Although this exchange undoubtedly caused my aunt momentary embarrassment, she later delighted in telling the tale. From all appearances, my father's refusal to attend the dinner with the governor had not caused a serious rift. At any rate, my aunt's love for her youngest brother would forgive him anything.

The Ill-gotten Ham

*A*t a midday meal, which the family was enjoying, one person after another made comments like, "I believe this is the best ham I have ever eaten," or "It's been a long time since I tasted anything so good."

I noticed Aunt Bern kept deflecting this and changing the subject. All of a sudden my mild-mannered uncle-in-law, dressed in coat and tie for meals, looked straight at Aunt Bern and asked, "Bernice, where did you get this ham?"

Aunt Bern sought to evade the question with a light-hearted laugh and "I'll tell you later, Stuart."

Now, my uncle, suspecting something amiss, and also knowing the area's choicest supplier of hams, put down his napkin with emphasis and said in cool, measured tones,

Uncle Stuart Gillis

"Bernice, did this ham come from Jeb Simms' farm?" His usually warm blue eyes looked steely. Everyone was riveted and very still. Uncle Stuart's anger was something we rarely observed.

Aunt Bern, who seldom flinched, appeared a little unnerved as she began her explanation. However, in a firm voice she replied, "Well, Stuart, Mr. Simms did come by. The poor man kept insisting I take the ham. I thought he might break down and cry if I didn't, so I accepted. Besides, I thought if you didn't know where it came from, it couldn't matter."

With that, Uncle Stuart, a dignified circuit court judge, stood up. "You know that I have a strict rule about never accepting gifts. I'm trying a case involving that man's son beginning next Monday. It may be too late to get another judge to come in for that date. If so, I will just have to postpone the trial until I can find a judge." Then in his courtly manner, he said, "Ladies, please, excuse me," and left the table. We heard him get his hat from the hall closet and walk out of the house, meal unfinished.

Was Aunt Bern upset? With a wave of her hand, she said, "You all please continue eating. It can't hurt you to eat it." Then, she removed the ham from the table, taking it to the kitchen. When she returned, she happily reported, "Rebecca is delighted to take the ham home. Stuart won't have to see it again." As far as I know, the situation was never mentioned again between them.

Aunt Bern's Advice on Party Giving

July 15, 1950

My dear Niece,

I am so glad you are going to entertain your new friends at a buffet supper. That is the simplest way and people seem to enjoy the informality of it. Thank you for asking my advice on what to serve. I do not have much experience with such suppers, but can think of some dishes that might be appropriate and that can be fixed before your guests arrive.

But, speaking of the arrival of guests. The best advice I can give is to have the place lit up, some fresh flowers to greet people and you or you and Tom at the door to greet each person. Give them a big smile and act as if you have been doing nothing all day, but waiting for them, though you have likely been preparing for this occasion all week. Try not to wear yourself out with too many details, or you will be unable to perform the most important part of the evening—that is, the conversation. The guests should be entertained, but they will find the most entertaining thing your interest in them and what's happening in their lives. People do love to talk about themselves.

Now, you have them all seated, introduced to one another (if some are unfamiliar) and talking about some topic of the day, or if you are in a private conversation with one or two, talk about them. Now, you have established a nice atmosphere, perhaps served fruit juice or whatever you young folks like and you can escape to the kitchen to put the finishing touches on what you are serving.

Let me know how the party turns out. Try not to worry

Reminiscent of Aunt Bern's parties, a table for a select few prepared by Julie Shealy Smith, daughter of former DeFuniak Springs resident Mary Julia Bailey Shealy.

over every detail, as I think you are prone to do, my dear. You have to remain focused on the guests having a good time and they will not if they catch you uneasy and nervous. Get everything ready before hand, planned well with all serving dishes ready, each part of the meal ready to serve, except for heating the rolls and serving the dessert. By that time, you or Tom will have served the coffee, and you can take your time with the dessert. The guests are happily chatting away, having enjoyed a delightful supper.

I know you will be a successful hostess for you are lively and competent in planning and organization. Now, relax and begin to plan well ahead of the occasion. Oh, I would not invite more than three other couples at this your first dinner party. Wish I could be present.

With lots of love,
Aunt Bern

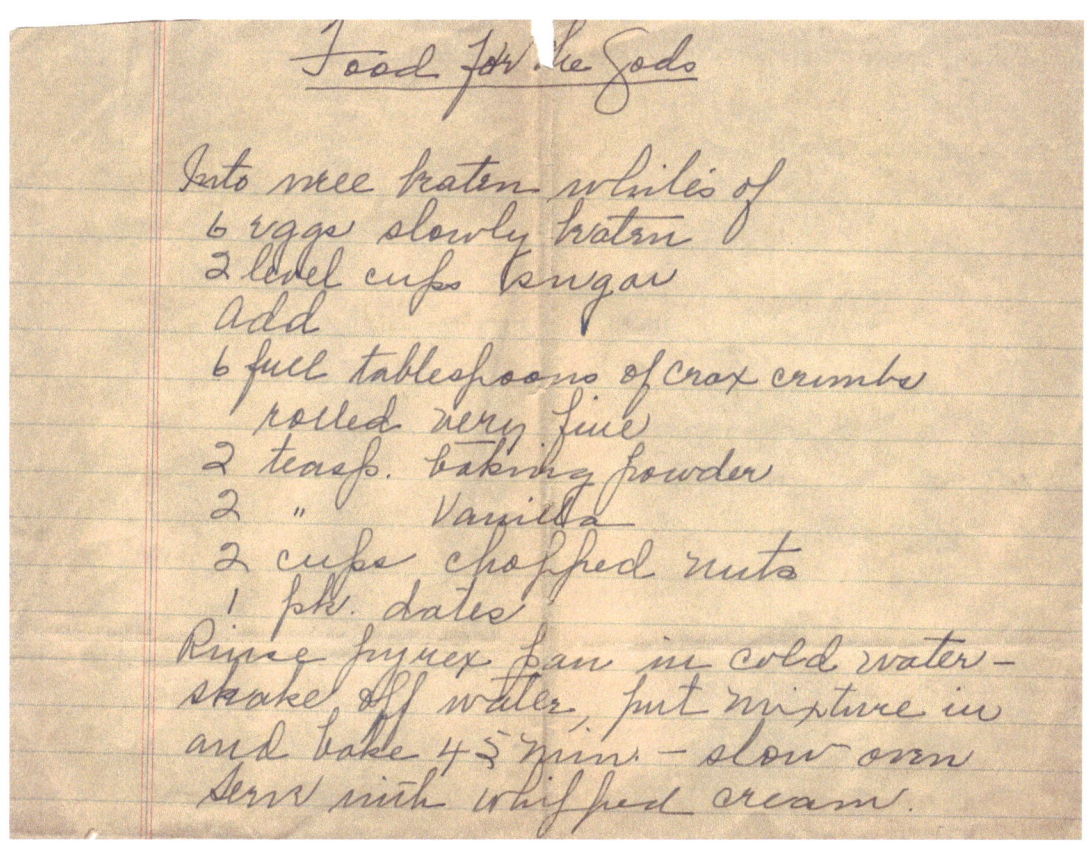

A winter recipe penned by Aunt Bern.

A TRIP TO TROY

Introduction

  Troy, Alabama, from the mid-19th and into the early 20th century, was considered a cultural center with its college, music and art classes, recitals and exhibits. It was geographically centered in South Alabama between the northern city of Columbus, Georgia, and the southern port of Mobile, Alabama. Grandmother Tatom's father, Urban Louis Jones, had initiated plans for a railroad connecting these two points with Troy at the center and which he expected would benefit the town economically. To raise money for this project, he and fellow investors borrowed money from New York banks.

  The railroad was halfway completed when the Civil War began. Both sides of that conflict in turn tore up railroad beds to prevent movement of supplies that could help the military. That ended hope for the railroad, but banks had to be repaid. In a paper by the Pike County Historical Society one reads exactly what the family had always said, that while the other investors refused to pay their share of the debt, Urban Louis Jones did. That meant that he lost local investments, land, money in savings. From this depletion he never recovered financially.

  The family is recognized by the historians of Troy as very influential. My great grandmother was a Murphree and her family was considered so special they have their own cemetery. When I heard Uncle Ira talking about the cemetery, I became eager to see it.

  I'd heard about Troy all my life, and so when Cousin Ethel wrote to invite us to visit along with other relatives, I was as thrilled as my mother in anticipation of the trip.

  Mamma got busy getting my sister Chris and me ready for the trip to Troy. We were schooled in how to behave in meeting elderly kin, on the proper way to sit in a chair (oh, the horsehair stuffing) and the correct way to handle a teacup. We were not to ask for cake or sandwiches, but to wait until it was offered. We would wear white gloves and have new hats, even though we were only ten and twelve.

The Story

On a hot summer day Mamma, Aunt Eleanor, my sister Chris and I drove the 150 miles to Troy. Upon our arrival at Cousin Ethel's house we were met with hugs and kisses from neighbors and relatives we'd never met. Invariably I was told, "My, how you've grown." I wondered how they knew that when they had never met me, or so I thought.

Cousin Ethel's house in Troy, Alabama

I was glad to meet Aunt Kitty, who did not insist on a hug and didn't stroke my head. Next to unwanted hugs and kisses, I disliked stroking, though I certainly didn't say so. Aunt Kitty was Cousin Ethel's mother and a sister of my grandmother Tatom. She was in her 80s but didn't act as I supposed people that old would.

We were informed that Mamma's sisters-in-law, Bessie and Mabel, would be arriving soon for supper. I looked forward to seeing them. Both had relatives nearby. I knew Aunt Mabel who had visited us in DeFuniak Springs. She and her husband, Dr. Lothair Tatom, and family had also once lived in DeFuniak. Dr. Tatom was apparently highly regarded and the family popular. Aunt Mabel had taught me to crochet, how to make a cat's cradle with string, and initiated my interest in poetry. The poem of Aunt Mabel's that I liked best was about Florida and entitled "Sand in my Shoes." She had a wry sense of humor that always brought smiles.

I knew Aunt Bessie only from pictures as the widow of Mamma's brother, Louis Tatom. On many Sunday afternoons I'd looked at the headstone of his grave when Mamma took flowers to the graves. The headstone gave his age as thirty-six when he died. Family lore had it that his death had occurred as a result of eating "bad oysters." I always wondered who had given him the bad oysters and if anyone else died. At the time he was living in Hosford, Florida, not far from famous Apalachicola Bay and the Gulf oysters were plentiful and should have been fresh. None of these questions has been answered. Aunt Bessie was left with four little children, all of whom had very successful careers serving in the military or marrying a military man. Everyone enjoyed hearing Aunt Bessie tell about her sons, Louis, John, Eugene, and daughter, Ann. Ann had been an officer of her freshman class at Florida State. Each of the men attained high ranks as officers in the Army and Navy, with Ann's husband serving on General McArthur's staff.

Cousin Ethel showed us to our rooms and said, "Make yourselves comfortable. Call me if you need anything. I'll see about supper, which should be in about thirty minutes."

My recollection of the evening was one full of stories and laughs and reminiscences. With the exception of Aunt Kitty and Cousin Ethel, the others had all lived in Geneva, Alabama, and each asked about some family or person. All knew something about Troy and events conveyed to them by my grandmother Tatom. And Aunt Eleanor had been born in Troy. Today, I wonder what my grandfather's work was in Troy in the 1800s before the family moved to Andalusia and then to Geneva.

Aunt Kitty was asked what it was like to be the first female student at Troy State College. As I recall, she had no stories of discrimination, only admiration for her desire to get a college education. Most of the young women her age, including my grandmother, had married early. My grandmother later regretted that she was home tending to babies as she watched her friends going to parties and to school.

That night in Troy affirmed most of what I'd heard about family prior to the trip. I loved all the conversation. What I did not hear was anything about the Murphree cemetery. Mamma's brother, Ira, had created a huge interest for me in that cemetery by his jokes and perhaps expectancy to be buried in Troy's family cemetery. I hoped next day we would get to visit the Murphree cemetery.

Next day after church, we sat on the front porch a while before Mamma announced it was time to visit some of our elderly kin and friends of her parents. From large house to large house we sat on uncomfortable chairs, sipped warm lemonade, and listened to the ladies talk. I don't believe there was a single man present at these visits. I don't recall now how many people or houses we visited, but it seemed endless. My mother enjoyed it all. Talking about her parents and the recollections of them made her happy.

Arriving back at Cousin Ethel's house, we joined all the aunts, Eleanor, Mabel, Bessie and great aunt Kitty on the wide porch. As Chris and I removed our hats and gloves, someone asked, "Well, what's the news of the aristocrats?"

"Bessie, don't start making fun of those old ladies. Remember we are kin to most of them."

Turning to us, Aunt Kitty said, "Girls, would you like some cold lemonade?"

"Yes, ma'am," we enthusiastically replied.

Speaking to her daughter, Aunt Kitty said, "Ethel, get these lovely girls a cold glass of lemonade. They deserve it and more for going with their mother to see all those old, complaining ladies."

"And, Ethel, while you're at it, ask Ruby's girl Evelyn to come out." As Cousin Ethel left, Aunt Kitty continued, "I want you all to meet her. Went all the way to Chicago and got herself a good job. Comes down here in the summer to see her folks. She is one fine young lady."

As the tall, well-dressed Negro girl approached, Aunt Kitty began to tell of her accomplishments. "You all know this girl's mother, who has been with me for thirty years. And I got to see Evelyn here growing up. Smart? This child was so smart they couldn't find enough books to suit her when she was in fourth grade."

Evelyn looked embarrassed but poised. She replied, "Miss Kitty, you know it was you who insisted I graduate from high school and then college. I likely never would've gone so far without your encouragement and help."

Mamma, seeking to relieve Evelyn's unaccustomed center stage position, went over and shook Evelyn's hand. "Evelyn, you are a credit to all the colored folks and white folks in Troy and South Alabama. What is it you do in Chicago?"

"I work in the Social Services just begun by President Roosevelt. We determine who needs assistance and who doesn't. You would be surprised at the large number of white people who come to us for help. So many people out of work."

"And, my dear, do you make the decisions about white as well as colored people?" Aunt Mabel asked.

"Yes, ma'am, we do. President Roosevelt, or maybe it was Mrs. Roosevelt, made sure that colored and white people were considered the same."

"Well, I do declare," replied Aunt Kitty. "Now isn't that amazing? I tell you I'm glad I voted for Franklin Delano Roosevelt."

With that, conversation began in smaller groups of twos and threes and Ruby's daughter retreated to the kitchen to help her mother prepare the dinner.

Aunt Kitty was a contemporary of the ladies we had visited. She was one of them but didn't want to be so identified. As the first female student at Troy State Normal School, she felt somehow superior to the women engaging in living room conversations about other people. However, she didn't leave the porch while her own folks shared information about family and friends.

Conversation went something like this: "Do you remember the day William Chapman came calling on Ethel carrying a bouquet of corn and greens?"

Midst laughter at this recollection, someone added, "Bill was quite a joking man. Wasn't their wedding beautiful?"

"Ethel was beautiful," another added.

"Eleanor, what was the last you all heard of your uncle Billy Jones? And do you know the real reason he went so far away—to California?"

Aunt Eleanor replied, "I suppose it was because of his leaving the Baptist church to become a Unitarian/Universalist minister. Mamma had a letter from him before she died. He and Aunt Alice seemed to be very happy. That was the last we heard. They loved California, the climate and the people of his church."

When no one offered anything further about what was to them strange behavior, the conversation moved to another part of the family. In hushed tones it would be something like this: "Poor Lizzie, staying home all those years with one child after another, nine in all, while her doctor husband ruled the roost and was so jealous she was forbidden to go anywhere without him, even to church. Do you know she was not even allowed to attend the Ladies Missionary Society?"

"I declare, that was terrible, but look at Lizzie now."

"Yes," Mamma would say, "Aunt Lizzie's out in the world now riding the Greyhound bus all over the country visiting her children. She is remarkable to take the bus, and without anyone going with her, to places she has never been.

"But why doesn't Lizzie get someone to drive her to take the train? She should have more comfort than riding a bus," one of the aunts would offer indignantly.

"Well, let's not criticize Lizzie; goodness knows she went through enough of that when Dr. Smart was alive."

"I guess one should not say it, but isn't it nice that he died first, just in time for Aunt Lizzie to do as she pleases?" That brought soft laughter as everyone seemed to be imagining Aunt Lizzie having such a good time traveling.

When I realized it was getting late and no one had mentioned the Murphree cemetery, I asked, "When will we see the Murphree cemetery?"

"Oh, my dear, why would you want to see the cemetery?" Aunt Kitty asked.

"Well," I responded, "Uncle Ira said it was so special that anyone buried there would certainly get to Heaven."

That brought laughter and Aunt Mabel saying, "That Ira, what he said was, 'If being buried in the Murphree cemetery will guarantee me an entrance to Heaven, then please take me there.'" More laughter.

Mamma added, "You know, Ira always finds humor in anything. He also made great fun of the family coat of arms, saying 'It looks to me like two blue buzzards and an old hound dog.'"

Aunt Eleanor offered, "My daughter, Florrie, in Jacksonville has joined the D.A.R. and that took inquiry into our ancestors. Then I believe Clarice, your daughter, Mabel, became interested."

"That's right," Aunt Mabel said. "Puzzles me why anyone would want that, but she did. I know some of the folks here are members of the United Daughters of the Confederacy, but I am not a joiner of that either."

The Murphree family monument (in 2005)

"Well, I think that if women want to belong to these organizations, that's fine. It gives them associations and social events, that is if they don't have to work," my mother said. And, for the first time, I realized my mother might prefer to do other things than to give daily piano lessons.

All this conversation had left the Murphree cemetery. I didn't get to visit it then or on another trip in the 1980s, when I too began to search for long dead ancestors and their kin. Mainly I was looking for some explanation for one of the closing remarks that I recall on that summer afternoon in Troy on Cousin Ethel's porch. Aunt Mabel suddenly said, "Here come the Black Dutch." No one came walking in, but who were they? I still ask questions, though I learned a lot on that trip to Troy.

Possible Explanations for the Term "The Black Dutch"

*I*t was on a front porch in Troy, Alabama, that I first heard the term "Black Dutch" used to announce the arrival of visitors. "Here comes the Black Dutch," said one of the aunts. At the time, it was jut an unusual phrase. But years later, I began to ponder its meaning. The gentlemen visitors were Vocius, Lotan and Cap (short for Casper) Jones – all apparently related to our Jones part of the family.

Why, I wondered all those years later when I heard the term to describe the Irish, were these men in Alabama dubbed the "Black Dutch"? And then there was the time when, filling out an application to attend Florida State, I asked my mother the background of my ancestors, and to the familiar Scotch/Irish/English, she added, "Remember the Dutch." I do not know why at that very point I didn't ask for an explanation. Perhaps I was too excited about going off to school to be interested in any answers.

What I have discovered is that there are so many explanations for the term that I suppose one could simply decide which one fit better the Joneses of Troy. Announce what caused these men to be labeled the "Black Dutch" and move on.

But first, let me share with you what I've learned, courtesy of the Internet and a personal conversation.

One theory of the origin of the term "Black Dutch" is that Dutch colonists who went to what is now Indonesia (then the Dutch East Indies) married native women and took them and their children back to Holland; there they remained, gradually melding into the larger community. A man from Amsterdam gave me that explanation.

Another explanation is that those designated "Black Dutch" were the result of Sephardic Jews from Portugal and Spain marrying Dutch women to escape the Inquisition. Their children then had dark skin, hair and eyes. Back of that theory is the historical fact of Spain's domination of Portugal, conscripting Portuguese men into its army and sending them as an occupying force into Holland.

There are other explanations, but these two seem the most likely to be accurate descriptions. One encounters other immigrant groups being assaulted with a term meant to insult. Thus, prefacing identification of an ethnic group with the word "Black" turns it into a derogatory declaration. In my wondering about the origin of "Black Dutch", it never occurred to me that this was meant as a slur, but rather a means of identification. Therefore, I shall continue to think of it as a means of saying that that person or group is distinguished by the dark color of skin, hair and eyes. Black indeed becomes beautiful.

THE MANY SUITORS OF NANCY TATOM

Preface

Miss Nancy Tatom

Nancy Ellen Tatom was one of eight children born to Abel and Eleanor Key Stokes Tatom. She was next to youngest, born in 1844, seventeen years before the start of the War Between the States. The darling of the Tatom family, she was beautiful and talented.

Her parents were from different backgrounds, though both families had been in America prior to the Revolutionary War. Her father was from Virginia, from a prominent family, but of moderate means; mother from a very wealthy, landowning family living the storied social life of well-to-do farmers. How, they met, I do not know. From family lore, Abel parted with the Church of England, having been influenced by the Wesley brothers, who established the Methodist Church. Where my great-grandparents first made a home, I also do not know. From Abel's ordination papers, it appears they lived initially in South Alabama. The Methodist Church moves its ministers about, which accounts for the several places of residence.

Cotton Valley, Alabama, is the address on several of the letters addressed to Nancy. A teacher's contract issued to Nannie lists Macon County as her place of employment. The small towns in Macon County are just north of her parents' home—at that time in Union Springs. Cotton Valley no longer exists as a town or a village. It was in what is known as the Black Belt because of the color of the soil and its richness. There also were large plantations in that area with the African-American (slave at that time) population dominating the census records. The small towns of Enterprise and Selma are a part of that once rich cotton-growing area. Today there is diversified farming, with peanuts the major crop.

It must have been difficult being the daughter of a Methodist minister, but it does not appear to have affected her invitations to parties. There is an invitation to the Cotton Valley

Calico Party. There would be dancing and lots of attentive young men. It is surprising that Nannie would be allowed to attend this occasion, inasmuch as her parents were very strict, and her older sisters had never been allowed such freedom. The daughters of Methodist preachers of that time knew the limitations of their social lives as a result of the good example demanded because of their father's position in the community. And, in the late 1800s, dancing was still frowned on by many in the Methodist Church.

My aunt Nannie won the hearts of many young men, as evidenced by the many, many letters remaining. My grandfather, A. Fletcher Tatom, was Nannie's youngest brother. When Nannie married, she left all the letters of former suitors in a trunk in her parents' keeping. It fell to my grandfather to take care of the parents until they died. They left behind trunks full of memorabilia. Among the keepsakes were Aunt Nannie's letters. And so here in Northern California in the first decade of the 21st century we can read the letters of adoration and pleading from several young men to a beautiful, young, independently minded woman.

In addition to Nannie's beauty, she was something of an artist, devoting lots of time to that, as well as for a time teaching school. There is a teaching certificate attached. There is a menu of a Christmas dinner to be served in Richmond, Virginia, ostensibly from one of her male friends. And there is an oil painting by Aunt Nannie hanging in our home.

Nannie married rather late for a young woman of that time. One supposes that the exciting social life and attentions of so many adoring young men influenced her marrying later than most young women. On the other hand, perhaps she simply hadn't met a man to whom she wished to be married.

On January 14, 1874, she was married to Benjamin R. Nix. On September 2, 1875, a son, Joseph Fletcher, was born to the couple. Four years later Nannie died, supposedly in childbirth. The family mourned her death with many stories of this beautiful girl. In my childhood I heard stories about Nannie as relatives gathered for summer visits.

Included in this account are a few of the many letters written to Miss Nannie by hopeful suitors. Note the effusive style, the words laden with adoration and love. We know nothing of what became of these gentlemen but marvel at the devotion and perseverance.

Introduction

On a lovely summer evening at our Gulf Coast Grayton Beach cottage, two of my maternal aunts sat on the porch in rocking chairs, enjoying the cool breeze with my mother and me. With the whooshing sound of the Gulf waves alternating with breakers and a bright moonlight, the ladies warmed to romantic tales of aunt Nancy, also called Nannie.

Only great aunt Lizzie, Grandmother Tatom's sister, was old enough to remember Nancy. Aunt Mabel was the widow of my mother's brother, Dr. Lothair Tatom. Mamma (Mamie Ruth) had thought it would be nice to have these aunts visit at the same time. And it was a compatible pairing. Both Aunt Lizzie and Aunt Mabel were forthright and sharply intelligent women who did not hesitate to express their opinions. Mamma and the aunts had all been reared in Alabama and knew many of the people and towns of South Alabama.

I loved lying in the hammock and listening to these ladies speak with much liveliness of days gone by when each of them had visited Grayton Beach, Florida.

I couldn't help getting into the conversation and asking aunt Mabel if the phosphorus in the water was as bright in the moonlight years ago as it was now.

"Of course, my dear. It's always present and always beguiling to lovers. How do *you* know about that bright light in the moonlight?"

A bit ruffled by aunt Mabel's direct question, I nonetheless said defensively, "You can't miss it. But I've only walked the beach at night with one boy."

"Ohhhhhhh!" exclaimed the aunts at once, increasing my discomfort. "Well," said Aunt Lizzie, "let's hear about it."

"No, ma'am. I'd rather hear about all those boy friends of Aunt Nannie's that one of you began to talk about when we came out on the porch."

The Story about Aunt Nannie

Aunt Lizzie, who had not talked much, said, "Well, I guess I am the oldest and the only one to have met Nancy Tatom. She was indeed extraordinarily beautiful and something about her caused anyone in her presence quietly to acquiesce to her. I met her at the home of Mamie Ruth's parents in Troy. Nancy came to visit the newlyweds, and they made sure all the kin met this young beauty, who was also an artist. I'd heard about all the men who had pursued Nancy and her refusals of proposals for marriage. Not many women experienced that much attention. But when you met Nancy, it became clear why she so attracted men. She was not only beautiful, but sweet, very bright and, at the same time, quietly elusive. My goodness, I have certainly rattled on too much."

"Not at all, Aunt Lizzie," Mamma said. "I've read many of the letters she saved. They are in a trunk of Papa's family letters. I guess because he took care of his parents, all the letters and memorabilia were left in those trunks. I've often wondered, though, why Nannie kept the letters and left them with her parents. There are dozens of them from different gentlemen, all most gracious and flowery and in beautiful handwriting, beseeching

> Atlanta April 7th 1871
>
> Miss Nannie,
> I trust that you will not think me bold in thus addressing you after so short an acquaintance, but so constantly has your image been before me since my return, and so importunate has been my heart pleadings to cultivate an acquaintance formed under auspices so favorable that I could no longer resist. I might be disposed to doubt a favorable reception of this were it not that I am a firm convert to the doctrine that "Our doubts are traitors, and make us lose the good we oft might win by fearing to attempt." Let this be my excuse and let it plead for a favorable consideration of the request that I may be allowed the pleasure of a correspondence with you. Hoping to receive a reply soon that will set at rest all doubt.
> I remain very truly your friend
> B. T. Turner

Nannie for permission to see her or to write."

"I've read a few, too," I offered, "and my favorites were Mr. Turner and Mr. Rutherford. But who wrote the poem addressed to Miss Nancy Tatom that begins with 'I had last night sweet dreams of thee.' Who wrote that poem?"

"If it's not signed, there's no way we can tell," Aunt Lizzie said. "I don't recall all the gentlemen who were in love with her. I just know there were many she rejected, and some of the family got afraid she would never marry."

Aunt Mabel spoke up with a recollection of the sisters of Aunt Nannie. "You know, her older sister Eliza never married, devoting her life to religion and a pious life. Her father must have been the influence there."

"Yes," Mamma added, "there's a letter from Eliza to her sister Martha, warning her of the temptations of a lesser life than devotion to the church. She urges Martha to remember the example and teachings of their parents and not to succumb to the excesses of the plantation crowd, who she feels lead a sinful life."

"What interested me when Mamie showed me the letters," Aunt Lizzie said, "was an invitation to a dance. Now, I am certain that the daughters of Methodist ministers in 1872 were not allowed to dance. Yet I suspect Nannie went to that dance or Calico Party. Somehow she was able with her wiles and beauty to gain her parents' permission."

"I'd love to see that invitation. Did you bring it, Mamma?"

"Yes, honey, go find it in the folder where I usually keep music. Why not bring out all the letters I brought to show everyone."

"Okay. Here it is. Let me read the invitation and see if you knew any of the gentlemen or their families. It says *"CALICO PARTY* by the young gentlemen

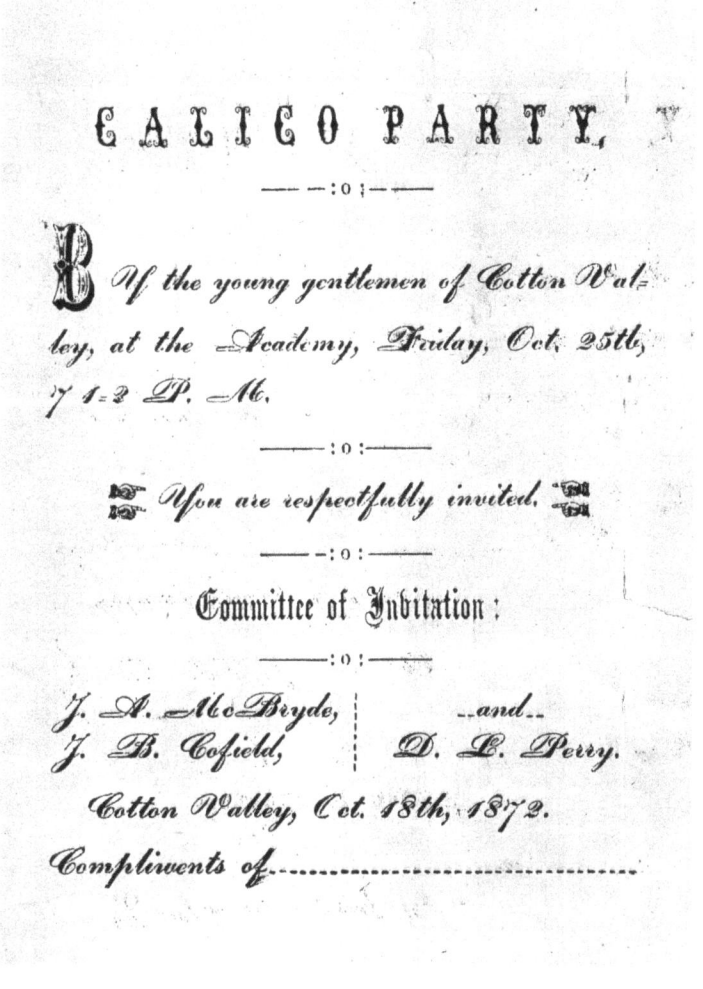

of Cotton Valley, at the Academy, Friday Oct. 25th, 4-8 p.m. You are respectfully invited. Signed: J. A. McBryde, J. B. Cofield, D. L. Perry. Cotton Valley, Oct. 18th, 1872."

The aunts began to speculate on the names of the men, but none knew them, except that the name McBryde was familiar as one of the Troy families with a house at Grayton Beach.

"Next time we see them, we'll inquire," Mamma added.

"Does anyone know how Nannie settled on Ben Nix?" Aunt Mabel asked.

"Does anyone know what happened to Mr. Nix?" Mamma asked.

"It's a familiar name, but I never knew him," responded Aunt Lizzie. "Union Springs, I think, was where they were married. It isn't that far from Troy, but somehow it was just far enough that we didn't keep in touch."

"It's a pretty up and coming place, I understand," said Mabel.

"Well, if her father was a preacher there, I am sure it was. He always went to prosperous towns," said Aunt Lizzie.

"I suspect that was due to the influence of his wife, who was from a well-off family in LaGrange, Georgia." Mamma was quoting a distant cousin with whom her sister had corresponded. "Perhaps Aunt Nannie and Mr. Nix made their home in LaGrange, since I think the Nixes also were from LaGrange."

"Anybody want to hear a letter from Mr. Z. T. Turner?" I asked.

"Okay," was the unanimous reply. I think Aunt Mabel may have known Mr. Turner in South Alabama.

"There's a letter from Mr. Rutherford begging Aunt Nannie for attention. Shall I read it?" I asked.

"By all means, let's hear it, Marjorie," Aunt Lizzie declared. And so I read Mr. Rutherford's letter.

from Union Springs, Alabama, Nov. 13, 1871

Dear Miss Nannie,

I was very much disappointed in not receiving an answer to my former letter, and but for the fear of displeasing you, would have written again before now. You surely can spare a few minutes, from your darling art, to

Painting by Nancy Tatom

write a few lines to one, who would think it a joy unspeakable, could he gain the privilege of devoting his whole life to your service. I would it were in the power of words to express what I feel for you, but I fear it is not, for language has its limits, but sentiment, like eternity, has none. I have learned, but too well, to substitute your name for the name of all that is dear in this life, and for all that we hope for of happiness in that mystic existence that we are taught to believe in beyond the grave.

Miss Nannie, you know that I love you, but you cannot know how intimately that love has become, as it were, incorporated into my very being. It is part of my daily life. I can no more conceive the idea of living apart from this love, than after the powers of respiration have been suspended. I do not mean to say that, failing to gain your love, would put an end to my existence, for you know 'the heart may break yet broken live on,' but I do say that should I fail to win you for my own, I will ever feel that my entire life has been a perfect failure.

You are in deed and truth, in some respects, a guardian angel to me, and will ever be, so long as I have life and sense enough to appreciate your pure, and beautiful character. Excuse this rambling letter for I have not time to look over it for correction.

Yours truly and affectionately,
R. T. Rutherford

And he enclosed these lines of an old song:

WE PARTED BY THE RIVER SIDE

We parted by the river, the moon looked down on you and me,
The stars put forth their looks of pride, the river murmured to the sea;
The dewdrop kissed the blushing rose, the gentle winds did sigh,
A word broke nature's sweet repose, that fond word was good-bye.

Oh, tell me that you love me yet,
For oh, the parting gives me pain.
Oh, tell me that you'll not forget,
For we may never meet again.

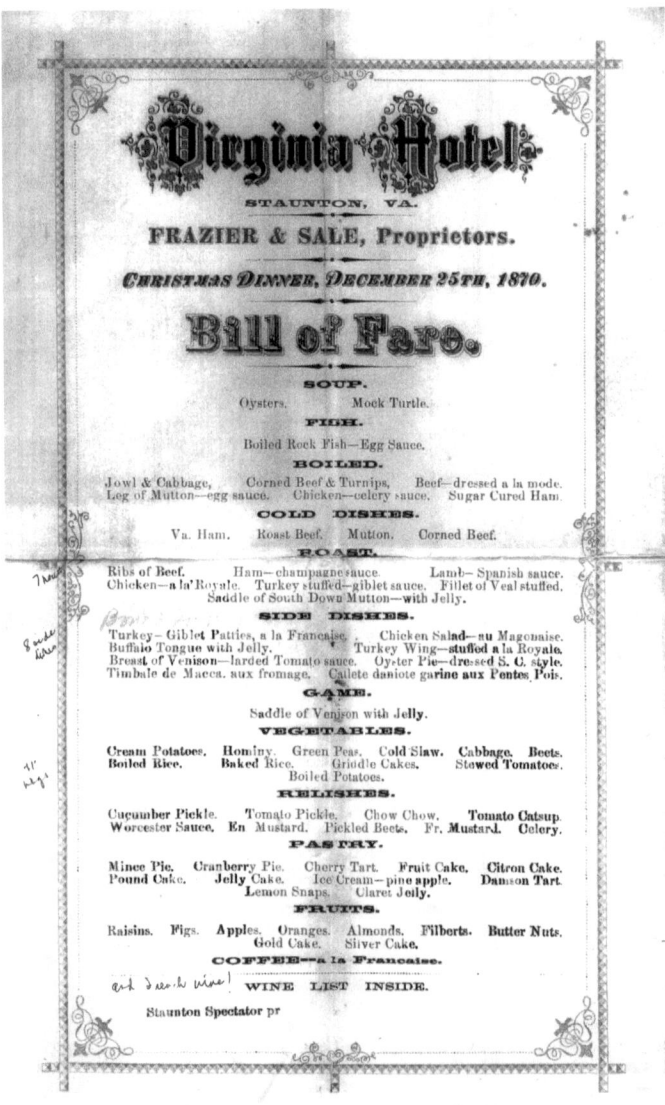

"Now, that's a passionate lover. How could Nannie turn him down?" Aunt Mabel said, not expecting an explanation from anyone present. I continued to look through the folder Mamma had brought with letters to aunt Nannie.

"I wonder if he was the one who was in school in Virginia and sent Nannie the menu from Christmas Dinner at the Virginia Hotel, December 25, 1870? Would anyone like to see what they had for dinner that day? Doesn't look to me as if the people in Virginia were suffering as much as the rest of the South. With a list of California wines and imported ones from Germany, France and Spain. I'll pass it around and you can all imagine the elegance of that dining room on Christmas

Day in Staunton, Virginia, the location of a military school."

"With all the attention she received even while pursuing her art and teaching, still she had time to communicate and entertain, and perhaps tease young men," Aunt Lizzie said.

My mother, always generous in her evaluation of persons, had this thought. "Aunt Lizzie, I think she may have tried to dissuade the men, but they were pretty persistent. And, did you see the teaching contract in 1871 for Macon County where she was paid thirty-five dollars a month? Hardly a living wage, even for those times. I think she pretty much had to stay with her parents until the right man came along."

"Mamie Ruth, you are the epitome of goodness. Here I was suspecting Nannie of encouraging men she really did not care for, and you present an entirely different picture of your aunt, my niece-in-law," Aunt Lizzie allowed.

"There's one last letter written to Nannie the year before her marriage to Ben Nix, with no signature. Here's the letter. See what you think of it."

Feb. 14, 1873

Will you read what I have to say? 'Tis but the simple second of a lost hope. If a hope that was born of the soul in an hour of joy and died as the present soul will die—if die it must—in sadness and gloom.

Let me recall to your mind for one brief moment a night that will ever be memorable. Then it was that I looked into a pair of dark, clear eyes, and thought I saw within their quiet depth, the index to a love that was all purity and goodness, all constancy and truth.

For some time after this, hope grew daily stronger in my heart, 'til I had come to believe in the reality of a picture, that seemed so fair.

Then, you left the Valley, and it seemed, for a time, that the light of my life was extinguished. But, even admit the darkness, the bright star of hope shone on in my heart, with its pure and steady light.

Time passed and I wrote to you. When day after day went by and no answer came, I doubted and troubled. I wrote again. I know not what. To this an answer came. Need I say what that answer contained? It was a cold and cruel letter, and it wounded a heart that loved you with a deep and passionate love. Few can appreciate the feelings with which it was read, for few, very few pass through the same ordeal. Though I still keep that letter, as a relic of a hope that is now dead, I never have, probably never will, open it again.

From that hour on, hope was dead and I determined to conquer the vain infatuation that gave it birth. I fought long and manfully. I shunned not only you, but all society. I even brought sin and folly—I shame to acknowledge it. Worn out at last, I felt that the conflict must end. I must see you or die. Now, I have seen you, and I know too well that hope can never be realized. I can feel the sweet though poisonous draught that it once offered to my lips still rankling in my veins. Yet I love you today with a strength that time can never abolish; and if the soul after death is permitted to return to any portion of its feelings—I must love you through all eternity. "Dien vous g order."

"Well," Aunt Mabel said, "if a man had come after me so ceaselessly, and without any encouragement, I would be pretty disgusted. Why can't he take the hints she's been giving him for years?"

"Mabel, if I had had a man who loved me so desperately, I would feel honored," replied Aunt Lizzie.

My mother, always seeing the good in every person, said, "Aunt Lizzie, you did have a man who loved you so much he didn't want to take a chance on any other man's getting interested."

"Mamie Ruth, I appreciate all Dr. Smart did for me. While he was alive, I didn't say anything, but I was in some ways a prisoner to his wishes and to his not allowing me even to go to church alone."

"I am sorry, Aunt Lizzie, that you were so isolated. But he did provide for you and the children generously," said Mamma, in defense of Lizzie's husband.

"Eight children kept me busy, so I didn't resent his being so authoritarian. Now when I see women doing so much more in community and even careers, I wish I'd had some of that opportunity. But then I wouldn't trade my family for anything…..so."

"You all are getting off the track of Aunt Nannie's rejection of that poor man who wrote the last letter. I wonder what became of him?" I asked.

Aunt Mabel turned to me and said, "Marjorie, you will just have to try and find out what became of Ben Nix, Mr. Turner, and Mr. Rutherford."

"Anybody for a walk on the beach in this beautiful moonlight?" the nineteen-year-old Marjorie asked.

They all agreed, and off we went for the walk that stimulated more conversation about love, real or imagined, faithful and unfaithful, rejection of lasting love.

Although some personal experiences were revealed, none of us had experienced the adoration expressed to beautiful, charming Nannie Tatom.

Contract with Teacher.

This Contract, by and between _Nancy E Tatum_ Teacher, and the School Trustee for District No. _23 & 24_, County of _Macon_, State of Alabama, (or Superintendent of Education for the County of _Macon_, State of Alabama,) witnesseth:

The said _Nancy E Tatum_ agrees to teach a Free Public School in District No. _23 & 24_, commencing on the _23rd_ day of _February_, 1871, for the term of _five_ months, and well and faithfully to perform the duties of Teacher in said school, according to law, and the rules legally established for the government thereof.

For and in consideration of said services, the said Superintendent of Education aforesaid, on behalf of said School District, agrees to pay the said _Nancy E Tatum_ the sum of _Thirty Dollars_ Dollars per school month, at the close of _each Quarter_ and to give such further aid as the law requires.

Witness our hands, this _Feb 21st_ day of _February 1871_ A. D. 1871

Nancy E Tatum .... Teacher.
P T Boyd .... Trustee.
Jos. Fitzpatrick

Approved:

A McBryde
Sup't of Education.

GOING TO THE GULF

Introduction

The first time I recall hearing about Grayton Beach was on a summer night on our front porch in DeFuniak Springs. My mother and father were reminiscing about the times they had enjoyed at the Gulf beach. Mamma was happy with the recollections. Daddy was talking about it, but not with much enthusiasm.

My mother talked about how beautiful the water and beach were when she and Daddy went there soon after they were married. They stayed at a hotel within sound of the surf, but set back one-quarter mile from the water's edge. Mamma laughed when she told about Daddy's reluctance to put on a bathing suit. Daddy replied that no self-respecting man would want to put on an ugly, scratchy thing like the embarrassing outfit one was supposed to wear to go swimming. "The things I do to please you!" But he too began to laugh. "I was a string bean with the suit falling off of me."

"Do you have pictures of that beach trip?" I asked, as I was now interested in what caused my father to be

Malcolm and Mamie Ruth Morrison at Grayton Beach circa 1921.

Frolicking at Grayton Beach

so disgusted with a bathing suit. The happiest times in my life as a child were whenever we went swimming, whether in the lake, at clear cold Ponce de Leon Springs, or the few times we had gone to the Gulf. And, although the bathing suit was wool and uncomfortable, it was worth a little discomfort to get in the water.

Getting to the Gulf beach in the late 1920s or mid-1930s was not easy. It took the better part of a day just to get to Grayton Beach, thirty miles from DeFuniak Springs. First one drove to Choctawhatchee Bay, from there took a ferry across the bay, and then drove over sandy, rutted roads about ten more miles to Grayton. Since this was a one-lane road, if one met another car or truck, the negotiation of backing up and finding a safe place to wait for the other to pass required diplomacy and a disposition of patience. This was not an easy trip.

But, oh, upon arrival it was beautiful. Sky and sea and sand dunes were perfect. One could smell the sea from about a mile away with the wind off the Gulf blowing inland. The last mile of that journey was always exciting, with the anticipation of fun in the surf, picnics on the beach, and moonlit nights lying on blankets looking at the stars.

By the late 1930s, a bridge across Choctawhatchee Bay had been completed, roads paved, and the trip from DeFuniak Springs to Grayton took a little over thirty minutes.

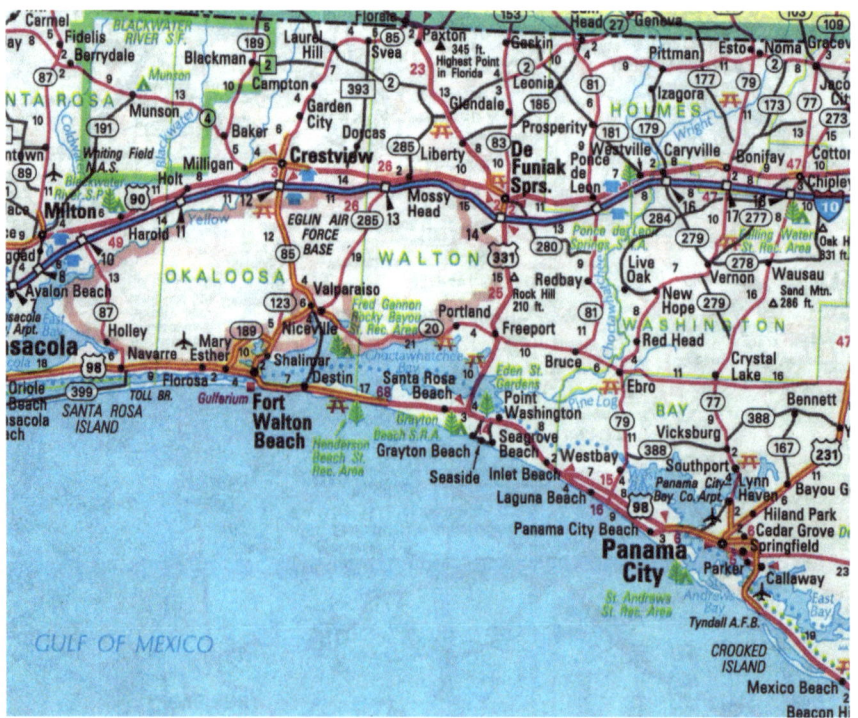

Mamma's Story

The first story about Grayton Beach is a recollection of my mother's experience as a child living in Geneva, Alabama, just above the Florida line. I heard this account often. As a matter of fact, Mamma repeated this story each time we approached Grayton Beach in the 1930s and 40s. Here's the account:

Every summer the family would go by carriages and wagons through the woods to the ferry crossing. From there, they traveled through more wooded area with a road roughly outlined in the sandy soil.

Every summer, Mamma said, her father would designate Jack, a highly respected African-American man, to take charge of getting my grandmother and the children to Grayton Beach. Having made this trip a few times before, Jack "knew the way."

One night had to be spent enroute. No hotels or motels along the way. The group camped out in the woods where bears and panthers still roamed, along with smaller animals like foxes. Mamma said no one was ever afraid with Jack in charge. There were servants to prepare the food and makeshift beds in the wagons. At night around the fire, there was singing of spirituals and age-old songs familiar to all.

Upon arrival at Grayton Beach, the house had to be opened, the pump primed,

kerosene lamps filled, beds made, the evening meal prepared. The children raced to the water's edge and impatiently waited for one of the adults to join them and give permission to go in the surf. Supervision of the children usually fell to one of the older daughters-in-law of my grandmother.

Occasionally, Jack himself wandered down to the water and gave the signal to go swimming or get out.

At that time, there were only a few houses at Grayton. With the exception of the Butlers, who owned much of Grayton Beach, all the other houses were occupied only for summer vacations. All the food had to be brought in, except for fish, which Jack provided with his skill as a fisherman. Catching of the plentiful crabs usually became a family outing, with even the children included in handling the nets. I believe Mamma said that my grandmother and Jack took turns with cooking the main meal. Such mutual tasks would not likely have taken place in Geneva.

Grayton Beach cottage

Marjorie's Stories

First Visit to Grayton Beach

Because of the early exposure to my mother's wonderful accounts about Grayton Beach, I was very excited when Mamma, my sister Chris, and I were invited to spend a week at Grayton Beach with a friend of my mother. My father had died earlier that year, so this thoughtful invitation was a wonderful escape from the sadness felt in our home. The friend had a cottage atop a sand dune with a panoramic view of the sea and beach. On this wide beach the house was about a quarter of a mile from the water, while the house of my mother's childhood experiences was set back three-quarters of a mile.

Hurricanes were not unfamiliar to the early residents and caution was used in the selection of location and the building of houses there. The house of our memorable stay was one of the first, if not the first, to be that close to the Gulf.

I have never forgotten the sudden revelation of beauty as we walked over a sand dune to the house. Sky and sea melded. The blue water with a touch of aquamarine against the blinding white sand caused me to stop and behold this scene in silence.

Chris, Marjorie, and Mamie Ruth Morrison at Grayton Beach

The thrill of hearing crashing waves is so familiar that I can almost imagine I am back there sitting on a sand dune or lying in bed listening to the rhythm of the waves. The sound ranges from a repetitious, dependable boom as the waves it the beach to one of softly whooshing, sleep-creating might of the sea.

This initial visit of several days and nights was filled with laughter, races up and down sand dunes, eating seafood, and Milky Way candy bars after a couple of hours spent sunning on a beach towel or swimming in the gentle surf.

Chased by a Hurricane

Once in the late summer, when we were at Grayton Beach, the sheriff's deputies came by and warned us to leave as they had information a "pretty big storm, perhaps a hurricane" was headed our way. We had no radio and, never having faced the situation, we delayed. "It can't be too bad," or so we said. "Besides, some families have decided not to leave." So we stayed and stayed before it was obvious we should leave.

We wandered down to the Gulf, as was our custom, for an afternoon swim, but mainly to look at the water and waves. Everyone was surprised at the sudden increase in the size of the waves. The wind too had become fierce. No more gentle breeze, but a punishing, loud giant. People began to talk of leaving the beach and driving inland.

Once that decision had been made, we very quickly packed up and joined the exodus. The only road left open was fast becoming impossible, according to the deputy who came by again as we were leaving. If we left immediately, he said, we might make it to the bridge crossing nearest us. The ferry was no longer making its runs across the bay. But we would have to take the beach road and that was a bit flooded.

We started out, my mother a newly licensed driver at the wheel. Although at thirteen I was a pretty good driver with more experience, Mamma wisely took over, not wishing to leave this responsibility to me. My mother, aunt Eleanor, sister Chris and I made it to the bridge with water lapping at the tires and wind such as we'd never before experienced. This was before hurricane warnings had become sophisticated enough for predictions and for people to know when they had to leave a beachfront area.

At the bridge, we were told only one car at a time could drive over the pontoon middle which had been quickly adjusted to accommodate people fleeing from the hurricane. In normal conditions this was an even part of the drawbridge that allowed boats through. Mamma took a deep breath. Chris and I in the back seat began silently to pray that Mamma could navigate us across the narrow middle section that we could see was up and down with the motion of the bay as it responded to the wind and waves.

When our turn came to drive across, Mamma's face was fixed with a desperate look, but she never hesitated to begin the hazardous drive. Although it only took a few minutes to drive over the pontoon, it seemed forever as the car moved forward, yet also up and down with the unstable middle section. We made it across and cheered once off the bridge entirely. Mamma didn't stop; she kept going through wind and rain until we reached our home in DeFuniak Springs.

Once there, at first she wouldn't get out of the car. We worried that she might have had a stroke and couldn't get out. She was just exhausted and empty of emotion from the strain of the drive. A brave woman. Many would not have had the courage to drive over that bridge, but the alternative was to seek shelter in someone's beach house, which surely would soon be as unsafe as what we faced.

Another Hurricane, Another Time

I must confess that another time, when on a house party with other sixteen- and seventeen-year-olds, I remained with the others when a storm was announced as "on the way." We knew it was reported as not being too strong, so we stayed and experienced the thrill of riding waves 8-9 feet high. The Gulf has gentle, low waves, not high surf of either the Atlantic or Pacific oceans, so this was a special challenge. It was very exciting and invigorating. Add to that the menacing look of dark, dark clouds and you have the picture of suddenly adventurous girls with boys eager to prove their strength. Where was our chaperone? I don't recall, but she was not swimming. Later, as dark descended, there were lots of expressions of "we should have left." By now it was too late to cross the bay.

We stayed up all night as the wind whined and whistled. We told ghost stories and made fudge candy. One after another of us looked down the street, straining to see reassuring lights in houses of others who remained there "riding out the storm." No telephone, no radio left us simply guessing what was happening. We had phoned our parents earlier while the only store was open and with considerable bravado proclaimed, "We are fine. It's only a storm."

Next morning we viewed the scene of sand dunes reduced in some places, while others increased in size by the shifting of sand. The Gulf had come up as far as the house closest to the water, but not to our house, about one-quarter mile back from the Gulf. The quiet following this tumultuous storm was eerie, and although we could have gone swimming, no one wanted to. In fact, I think we all left, happy to be going home to the security we had always known.

Uncle Ike's Story

One summer Mamma's brothers, Ike and Ira, arrived with their children to spoend a couple of days with us. Pallets were placed on the floor, cots were brought into bedrooms and onto the back porch to house the total of eight children. Half were in late teens, the other half were pre-teens. I think Chris and I stayed in a bedroom with Mamma and Daddy. Uncle Ike with Aunt Annalee. Perhaps Uncle Ira supervised the "kids" outside on the porch.

Everyone looked forward to a day at the Gulf beach. The uncles had brought with them a box full of cleaned coffee cans. I could not imagine why but soon learned. While we were swimming, Uncle Ike and Uncle Ira built a fire on the beach, placed a huge pot on the fire and began to stir what became a seafood chowder. (We had stopped at a familiar icehouse that also sold fish, shrimp and crabs.) As we approached the fire, towels drawn over our wet bodies, the chowder smelled better than any seafood I had ever had.

The uncles began to serve the chowder in the coffee cans. Chris and I passed the crackers and buttered bread and cheese, which had been kept cold in the ice chest. Awaiting us was the chocolate cake Mamma had made the day before. My father, observing the preparations for this meal at our house in DeFuniak Springs, had commented on all the fuss over a beach picnic. He was not going with us because he really did not enjoy the beach, its informality and sitting on the sand. I thought of Daddy and all the fun he was missing. Everyone there was enjoying this delicious treat and the beautiful setting. No one else was to be seen on the beach.

The evening concluded with the older girls leading us in songs and singing games that got everyone moving and laughing. From time to time I had to look at the gorgeous sunset, my favorite time of the day anywhere but especially at the beach. Being with the Tatoms on that afternoon and evening remains a very special time in my memory.

Cousin Kay Gets a Close-up View of a Whale at Grayton Beach

One of the most exciting events in all the years of our going to Grayton Beach occurred when a very large whale was discovered beached not far from where people usually swam. It was a huge curiosity as whales were not often seen in the Gulf waters. There was lots of speculation on what had caused the whale to beach itself. Soon, however, there was consensus that the whale had become sick, perhaps lost its way and now was dead. Prior to that, men tried to push it back into the water, in hopes it would revive, only to have the waves bring it back onto the shore.

While it was still offshore, anyone with a boat was rowing or sailing out to view it better as sharks circled round. My cousin Kay was visiting us and had become acquainted with a young man we didn't know. While we were watching the commotion surrounding the whale, all of a sudden my sister spotted Kay riding in a motor board at top speed and fast approaching the whale and the small crowd of boats. It appeared they would crash into either the whale or the boats, when all of a sudden the man at the wheel turned sharply and steered out to sea.

My mother, who had been very cautious about Kay's activities and safety in the water, was very upset that Kay was with an unknown man in a motorboat heading for no one knew where. Meanwhile, Kay was having a wonderful time in this speed boat. My mother, sister and I began to yell and wave to the man and Kay, but they kept going now parallel to the shore but too far out to hear us calling "Kay, come in, come in."

Later, when my cousin did appear, she apologized for any worry she caused my mother, whose appearance indicated her condition. Kay, seeking to make amends, said, "Mamie, he's a senior at the University of Alabama and a member of the Sigma Chi." That seemed to make him a reliable person in her view, but not in Mamma's. Somehow belonging to a fraternity did not impress, or that he went to the University of Alabama.

This was the first time in my life, then or later, that I heard my mother issue an edict. "Katherine Stuart, your parents have entrusted me to take good care of you. I can't do that if you go off without my knowing where you are going or with whom. You are not to see this young man alone again while you are here at Grayton Beach."

"But, Mamie, I'll be here another two days and he's staying another week. He really is a nice guy."

"I'm sorry, Kay," Mamma added, "but I must have your promise you will not go anywhere again without consulting me, and if it is with that boy, it is no. He has demonstrated he is reckless by the way he approached a crowd of people in boats with sharks circling and then flying off at high speed. No, he is not trustworthy."

"What will I tell him? He asked me to meet him tonight at the dance at Van's store."

"That's fine, if you stay indoors, dancing, or having some refreshment."

And my cousin did just that. She might have wanted to wander the beach in the moonlight, but she knew she had to obey or else there would be trouble when she arrived home.

In my mind, this happening at Grayton Beach remains one of the most unforgettable times, though it was not a major event in Kay's life. She loved fast cars, motorcycles and now motorboats. However, she often expressed regret that she had so worried my mother. The whale remained in a state of decay for days, the poor thing knowing no privacy. I don't know who finally carted off the remains. I do know this story was repeated many times, both for my cousin's daring and because a whale in those Gulf waters was so rare.

Often Repeated Tales of Events at Grayton Beach

Going crabbing at Destin

Summer after summer a popular story was the one about Cousin Dave's taking our household, of my mother and her two daughters, his son, and a neighbor's visitors from the North—all of us in two vehicles—to Destin to catch crabs. One vehicle was a pickup truck. This was a first for my sister and me—to ride in an open pickup truck in the darkness just before dawn.

Cousin Dave had said we had to get up early to get to Destin when the tide was coming in (or was it when it was going out?). That seemed to give the driver of the truck license to speed, and so we did, meeting no other cars. A very warm July early morning just at dawn was so beautiful I momentarily lost all interest in catching crabs but instead loved looking at the sky.

Once at East Pass, where the Gulf enters the bay, people scrambled out of cars and the truck, unloading crab nets, rushing to get to the shoreline. I too grabbed a crab net and half ran with the others.

In less than two hours the group had caught 90 crabs. And it had been exciting chasing crabs, so plentiful that one did not know which one to follow through the shallow, very clear water.

Of course, no crabs were wasted. Each of us took crabs from door to door to the beach community of Grayton, and the people enjoyed a delicious lunch or dinner from our catch. The startling fact of so many crabs in the 1940s and hardly any a few years later caused this to be a popular story in the latter part of the 20th century. "Fished out," old timers said with disgust.

Actually the diminishing of available crabs was noticed in the mid-1960s when my sister and I, with my son Tommy, age thirteen, discovered absolutely no crabs to be found in the same waters. We had told Tommy of the bountiful crabs he would catch if we got up early, as Cousin Dave had instructed us years before. To our great surprise, the trip was a complete disappointment. No crabs there and very little crab meat served in seafood restaurants along the Gulf Coast.

Much of the narrow strip of land between the bay and the Gulf had been covered with condominiums filled not only in the summer but with many year-round residents. Surely the land and water used by inhabitants of those buildings had put a strain n the natural habitat of all fish and crabs. Our favorite fish, Gulf snapper, was also scarce. An environmental movement was late in coming to the Gulf Coast as most people preferred to continue to build and hope for a comeback. Only a few environmentally conscious individuals pleaded for caution in developing the land at the expense of the natural beauty, and sadly they were ignored for the sake of making money.

East Pass, east of Fort Walton, connecting Choctawhatchee Bay with the Gulf of Mexico

Cousin Ethyl's Sunburn

Not once but dozens and dozens of times my sister and I and any young people who were visiting us heard about Cousin Ethyl's terrible sunburn.

"Girls," Mamma or Aunt Eleanor would begin, "you should not go out into the blazing sun. You could get very sick from sunburn."

Turning to any other adult relative present, one of them would say, "Tell them again about how sick Cousin Ethyl got from walking to Seagrove in the middle of the day, thinking since it was a cloudy day the sun would not bake her skin."

"Oh," some one of the adults would add, "Ethyl was a beautiful young woman, with alabaster skin. Honey, she was so beautiful, people would stop dead still just to look at her. But then she got sick from sunburn and spent days and days in bed with her mother keeping wet poultices of vinegar on her back."

"They said she cried much of the night from pain. It was many nights and days (I cannot recall how many) before Ethyl felt well enough to get out of bed."

"And wasn't she lying on her stomach much of that long siege?"

"That's right. It hurt too much to lie on her back. So, girls, please do not stay out too long, if you must lie in the sun. Remember what happened to Cousin Ethyl and do not suffer the same fate."

Escape from a Shark

In the spring of 1938 a group of high-school sophomores planned a weekend stay at Grayton Beach. As a semi-adult, the beauty of Grayton was ever more apparent than in childhood. Houses set back from the water's edge left the beautiful beach in a natural state with sea oats and grasses growing on the dunes. In March, unless there is an unusual "warm spell," few people swim. However, when a crowd of kids begin to dare one another, in they go, yelling all the way.

Five couples made up the group. The planners, mindful of the required chaperone, selected the mother of one of the girls. She was known to be easy going, not too demanding. After many hours of planning, the special Friday of their early vacation arrived. All went well the first night of the designated girls' preparing the meal, followed by either walks on the beach or fierce games of Scrabble.

Saturday morning the sun came out, the temperature was perfect for swimming, and all of us young people raced to the water's edge, tossing towels on the sand and running as we waded deep enough to swim. As we swam farther from the shore, the crowd narrowed to the real swimmers, of which I was one. My cousin, Lin, his girl friend, Peggy, and I continued to swim, crossing the sand bar and on out into deeper water.

Treading water, we turned to look at the group on the beach, now joined by a couple of men we didn't recognize. They all seemed animated about something. There were so few people at the beach on that weekend that we casually wondered who they were. "Just Alabama folks" was usually the answer to the identification of stangers. Probably fishermen, we assumed.

Suddenly, someone shouted to us, "Look out!" That's all we heard over the sound of waves breaking. Then everyone on shore began to jump up and down, with the men pointing out beyond us—and one making a sign with his hands. To me, it looked as if he was pointing a gun. Lin immediately realized they were telling us a shark was approaching. "Go, go, go," he yelled. We began to swim as fast as we could, but Peggy and I couldn't keep up with Lin's strong strokes. Somehow we made it to the sand bar, thought we were safe, and began to slow down. To our surprise and shock everyone continued to yell, "Get out!" We each glanced over our shoulders and saw the shark still pursuing us. Lin literally lifted both girls, one on either arm, and dragged us onto the beach.

Exhausted, we fell down onto the safe sand, as others watched the shark slowly retreat. No one had ever before seen a shark swim over the sand bar. Talk began immediately of what everyone had seen and what Lin had accomplished. How did he get the strength? What were we thinking? How did the girls manage to swim so fast? Through deep sighs, Peggy and I explained that, if you are being chased by a shark, you somehow get superhuman strength. I added, "It helps if one is lucky enough to have a strong swimmer like Lin nearby."

The size of the shark took over the conversation. One of the fishermen reckoned it had to be eight feet. The other one said that wasn't too big for a shark. And someone else added that any size shark is too big to be good company. The big question: "What was a shark doing in our waters in March?" That was unusual. No one had the answer.

When the excitement died down, the young people settled for sun bathing. No one was interested in swimming for the remainder of our visit. Bonfires on the beach, Monopoly, and dancing to records became the entertainment.

Marjorie Morrison and Tom Moylan

Aunt Bern's Visit to Grayton Beach

Aunt Bern had very specific likes and dislikes. While most of the members of our family loved the Gulf beach and vacationed there every summer, Aunt Bern refused to visit. Her negative response was, "My dear, I do not like sand. It gets in everything. I do not like to swim. That requires dressing and undressing, and besides there are too many fish like stingrays and sharks that are ready to assault one. But, thank you for inviting me."

We were happily surprised one summer when she agreed to visit us and attend a beach picnic. I can't recall what caused this turn-about. On the appointed day, Aunt Bern arrived, having driven herself over sandy roads, without complaint (women with Aunt Bern's strength do not complain). She had hardly been present fifteen minutes before she asked when the picnic would begin. She really had to get home early.

Rushing up the sandwich making, the household, giddy with the excitement of Aunt Bern's arrival, hastily got ready to walk to the beach. We were dressed in typical beach clothes. Aunt Bern kept on her shoes and stockings, her hat and gloves. She wore a lovely summer dress and carried a parasol.

No one laughed at the picture of Aunt Bern dressed as if for a garden party on the trek to the beach. Someone carried a canvas folding chair, realizing that Aunt Bern would never sit on a blanket in the sand, as we always did on beach picnics. I think my mother even considered taking china and silverware but then decided to use paper plates, as usual, with ordinary forks.

Everyone was aware of the urgency of finishing so Aunt Bern could go home. So, little conversation took place. My sister tried to get Aunt Bern to remove her shoes and feel the cool sand. Of course, that was refused, but kindly. Finally, the ordeal was over for all of us. We walked back to Aunt Bern's car, relieved that the long-hoped-for visit was over. Never again would the request be made to someone who really did not like surf and sand.

Moonlight Nights at Grayton Beach

There can be no more romantic place than a warm summer night accompanied by a gentle breeze and brilliant moonlight on the slowly moving waves at Grayton Beach. The waves come in with regularity and without the usual startling sound. Rather, the waves break at the last minute with a soothing whooshing sound.

The young people at Grayton Beach have strolled early across the wide stretch of white sandy beach to climb to the top of sand dunes. From that vantage point they are ready for the sunset show. The sky never disappoints. Streaks of red and gold and pink appear and remain for long periods of time. The picture is so awe-inspiring that voices are silent as people watch to the accompaniment of the soft surf. Later they will wander down the dunes to water's edge to feel the warm water of the Gulf on their feet as the gentle waves caress them.

When the moon is full, it has already made an appearance in the eastern sky and begun to move over the water. Slowly it brightens as sunlight vanishes and the glorious show begins. Again there is quiet, as in a cathedral, as the second show of the evening begins. This one will last longer—long enough to run home for a blanket on which to lay one's pleasantly tired body.

Swimming vigorously during the day has tired even young bodies. However, the plan is to experience this moonlight and star extravaganza while resting comfortably on a blanket with one other significant person. He will whisper his love for the girl while she tries to concentrate on the sky or point out the bright light of phosphorus on the breaking waves. Under the spell of the moonlight, and his persistence, she ceases to concentrate on the natural beauty and succumbs to his ardor, the kisses of the beloved friend.

They will return again and again to Grayton Beach, repeating the ritual of sunset and moonlight nights. Now they do not run home for a blanket; they take one with them to the beach. And they do not race up sand dunes but walk slowly to the top, believing the dunes have gotten higher in the preceding fifty years.

Sunset at Grayton Beach

Photo Credits

Sources of photos other than family photographs and those of individual persons provided by friends:

Preface:

Porches in DeFuniak Springs: The Walton Hotel, from an early postcard with no photographer identified; the Bruce/Rivard House with a July 4th view of the lake from *Florida Living Magazine*, 1986. The Duncan Gillis House, Knox Gillis House, Wesley House (now Eden State Park), by Tom Moylan. The McConnell House, *Victorian Homes*, 1992. The Morrison House, by Bev Clark, realtor. The Chatauqua Auditorium and aerial view of the lake, Williams Gallery. DeFuniak Springs, FL. First Presbyterian Church, *Florida Living Magazine*, 1986. DeFuniak-Walton Library by Frances Jones.

A Summer Night on the Porch:

Baldwin Avenue (main street) from early postcard with no photographer credited.

The Books Must Go:

John Newton, John Morrison, Alexander McCaskill, from *History of Walton County,* John L. McKinnon.

"Here Come the Yankees":

Ellen, from a tintype from the Morrison Family, courtesy of Fred and Sharon Wilharm, recent residents of the former Morrison home. Federals on deck of gunboat and Confederates at Pensacola: National Archives at College Park, MD.

The Much Traveled Confederate Monument:

The courthouse and monument from an early postcard.

The Mysterious Death of Uncle John

DeFuniak Springs railroad station, from an early postcard; station now renovated and serves as the museum of the Walton County Heritage Association.

Aunt Bern's Legendary Parties:

Tea party, *Southern Living Magazine*.

A Trip to Troy:

Cousin Ethyl's house and the Murphree monument in Troy, AL, taken by Eloise Murphree.

The Many Suitors of Nancy Tatom:

Photo of one of Nannie's paintings, by Kay Williams.

Going to the Gulf:

Photo of Hubert Graves' painting of a Gulf beach by Amina Al Jamal.

Grayton Beach cottage photo used by permission of owner Van Ness Butler.

Sunset photo by Tom Moylan.

Back cover:

Marjorie Moylan and friends: *San Francisco Examiner*.

www.ingramcontent.com/pod-product-compliance
Lightning Source LLC
Chambersburg PA
CBHW041536220426
43663CB00002B/53